Glenn Gould

Glenn Gould

by MARK KINGWELL

With an Introduction by
John Ralston Saul
SERIES EDITOR

EXTRAORDINARY
CANADIANS

PENGUIN CANADA

Published by the Penguin Group

Penguin Group (Canada), 90 Eglinton Avenue East, Suite 700,
Toronto, Ontario, Canada M4P 2Y3 (a division of Pearson Canada Inc.)

Penguin Group (USA) Inc., 375 Hudson Street, New York, New York 10014, U.S.A.
Penguin Books Ltd, 80 Strand, London WC2R 0RL, England
Penguin Ireland, 25 St Stephen's Green, Dublin 2, Ireland
(a division of Penguin Books Ltd)
Penguin Group (Australia), 250 Camberwell Road, Camberwell, Victoria 3124, Australia
(a division of Pearson Australia Group Pty Ltd)
Penguin Books India Pvt Ltd, 11 Community Centre, Panchsheel Park,
New Delhi – 110 017, India
Penguin Group (NZ), 67 Apollo Drive, Rosedale, North Shore 0745, Auckland,
New Zealand (a division of Pearson New Zealand Ltd)
Penguin Books (South Africa) (Pty) Ltd, 24 Sturdee Avenue, Rosebank,
Johannesburg 2196, South Africa

Penguin Books Ltd, Registered Offices: 80 Strand, London WC2R 0RL, England

First published 2009

1 2 3 4 5 6 7 8 9 10   (RRD)

LIBRARY AND ARCHIVES CANADA CATALOGUING IN PUBLICATION

Kingwell, Mark, 1963-
Glenn Gould / Mark Kingwell.

(Extraordinary Canadians)
Includes bibliographical references.
ISBN 978-0-670-06850-0

1. Gould, Glenn, 1932–1982. 2. Pianists—Canada—Biography.
I. Title. II. Series: Extraordinary Canadians
ML417.G69K55 2009   786.2092   C2009-902415-2

Visit the Penguin Group (Canada) website at **www.penguin.ca**

Special and corporate bulk purchase rates available; please see
www.penguin.ca/corporatesales or call 1-800-810-3104, ext. 477 or 474

This book was printed on 30% PCW recycled paper

CONTENTS

CONTENTS

INTRODUCTION BY

John Ralston Saul

How do civilizations imagine themselves? One way is for each of us to look at ourselves through our society's most remarkable figures. I'm not talking about hero worship or political iconography. That is a danger to be avoided at all costs. And yet people in every country do keep on going back to the most important people in their past.

This series of Extraordinary Canadians brings together rebels, reformers, martyrs, writers, painters, thinkers, political leaders. Why? What is it that makes them relevant to us so long after their deaths?

For one thing, their contributions are there before us, like the building blocks of our society. More important than that are their convictions and drive, their sense of what is right and wrong, their willingness to risk all, whether it be their lives, their reputations, or simply being wrong in public. Their ideas, their triumphs and failures, all of these somehow constitute a mirror of our society. We look at these people, all dead, and discover what we have been, but also what we can be. A mirror is an instrument for measuring ourselves. What we see can be both a warning and an encouragement.

These eighteen biographies of twenty key Canadians are centred on the meaning of each of their lives. Each of them is very different, but these are not randomly chosen great figures. Together they produce a grand sweep of the creation of modern Canada, from our first steps as a democracy in 1848 to our questioning of modernity late in the twentieth century.

All of them except one were highly visible on the cutting edge of their day while still in their twenties, thirties, and forties. They were young, driven, curious. An astonishing level of fresh energy surrounded them and still does. We in the twenty-first century talk endlessly of youth, but power today is often controlled by people who fear the sort of risks and innovations embraced by everyone in this series. A number of them were dead—hanged, infected on a battlefield, broken by their exertions—well before middle age. Others hung on into old age, often profoundly dissatisfied with themselves.

Each one of these people has changed you. In some cases you know this already. In others you will discover how through these portraits. They changed the way the world hears music, thinks of war, communicates. They changed how each of us sees what surrounds us, how minorities are treated, how we think of immigrants, how we look after each other, how we imagine ourselves through what are now our stories.

You will notice that many of them were people of the word. Not just the writers. Why? Because civilizations are built around many themes, but they require a shared public language. So Laurier, Bethune, Douglas, Riel, LaFontaine, McClung, Trudeau, Lévesque, Big Bear, even Carr and Gould, were masters of the power of language. Beaverbrook was one of the most powerful newspaper publishers of his day. Countries need action and laws and courage. But civilization is not a collection of prime ministers. Words, words, words—it is around these that civilizations create and imagine themselves.

The authors I have chosen for each subject are not the obvious experts. They are imaginative, questioning minds from among our leading writers and activists. They have, each one of them, a powerful connection to their subject. And in their own lives, each is engaged in building what Canada is now becoming.

That is why a documentary is being filmed around each subject. Images are yet another way to get at each subject and to understand their effect on us.

The one continuous, essential voice of biography since 1961 has been the *Dictionary of Canadian Biography*. But there has not been a project of book-length biographies such as Extraordinary Canadians in a hundred years, not since the Makers of Canada series. And yet every generation understands the past differently, and so sees in the mirror of these remarkable figures somewhat different lessons. As history rolls on, some truths remain the same while others are revealed in a new and unexpected way.

What strikes me again and again is just how dramatically ethical decisions figured in these people's lives. They form the backbone of history and memory. Some of them, Big Bear, for example, or Dumont, or even Lucy Maud Montgomery, thought of themselves as failures by the end of their lives. But the ethical cord that was strung taut through their work has now carried them on to a new meaning and even greater strength, long after their deaths.

Each of these stories is a revelation of the tough choices unusual people must make to find their way. And each of us as readers will find in the desperation of the Chinese revolution, the search for truth in fiction, the political and military dramas, different meanings that strike a personal chord. At first it is that personal emotive link to such figures which draws us in. Then we find they are a key that opens the whole society of their time to us. Then we realize that in that 150-year period many of them knew each other, were friends, opposed each other. Finally, when all these stories are put together, you will see that a whole new debate has been created around Canadian civilization and the shape of our continuous experiment.

People around the world sensed from the first moment they heard him that Glenn Gould was about much more than playing the piano better or differently. In what can be called chance or destiny, he emerged as part of a creative explosion of ideas and sounds in Toronto. Marshall McLuhan, Harold Innis, Northrop Frye, Glenn Gould. All of them were reflecting and experimenting on what communications would and could become in a very different era, and they were all doing this in the same place at the same time. What the twentieth and now the twenty-first century thought and thinks about how we communicate with each other began in that place with those people.

Mark Kingwell is a philosopher of our times and of our attempts to reinvent our existence. And he has long placed music at the core of his ideas. He is able to get at the mysterious effect Gould had upon us via what he did with sound or, as Kingwell puts it, with silence. And he has found a way to draw out of the Glenn Gould we all thought we knew an even more remarkable figure who, whether through sound or silence, reveals us to ourselves.

Glenn Gould

CHAPTER ONE

Aria

The voice: it is fast, precise, self-satisfied, a little pompous.

It is filled with awkward attempts at the wry aside, like the meander of a scholar who has been giving the same lectures too often, doing accents and delivering anecdotes too polished by previous telling. The voice is also ironic, amused, intelligent, resonant, mischievous. It is preoccupied with itself, but not evasive or merely self-indulgent. The speaker answers questions, relishing the thought of them, even questions deemed by the speaker himself to be fearful or intimidating.

There is crisp structure in the sentences, delivered in well-formed paragraphs, cogent and architectural. It is the music of Glenn Gould's spoken English, a cultivated Canadian accent from a half-century ago, a tone fled almost entirely from this nation now, the mixture of flat and orotund phonemes peculiar to the official culture of emergent nationhood, the language of the CBC, of diplomacy, of the academy. The consonants, especially t's and d's, are clipped—as indeed are the musical consonants of his characteristic lucid and precise playing.[1] The vocabulary is wide, though sometimes musicological or precious: *aleatoric, motivic, thereunto pertaining.* The word *film* has one and a half syllables.

For Glenn Gould, the structure of speaking and the structure of thought itself were codependent, the mind's cacophony disciplined into a precise line by finding the right word, the artful compound sentence. The same is true in his voluminous, sprawling body of written work. Most important, it was true in his thinking about and playing of music. Glenn Gould above all sought structure in music, the "skeleton" of a piece, revealed in his interpretations, which were sometimes disparaged as "loose" because they were less formal than the academic standard. But they were never actually loose, only novel—loose in relation to a master-sense of the work, perhaps, but never in themselves. Nor was there any looseness in the music of his talk, either in form or content.

Aleatoric means that aspect of music subject to improvisation or chance. The term comes from the Latin word *alea,* meaning dice, those rolling cubes of chance. It was introduced into music theory in the 1950s to describe the work of, among others, Pierre Boulez and Karlheinz Stockhausen, but it can be applied to much older music containing elements of randomness within larger structures. Glenn Gould, master of memory and technique, is not usually associated with improvisation in music, nor with these avant-garde masters; but the clue to understanding his music, and hence his mind, is contained here. For Gould not only played music, he played with it. He wanted to interpret a given piece so that it felt to the listener *as if he were making it up in the moment.* Achieving that effect required extraordinary measures of control and discipline, over himself and over as much of the world as he could command.

"For me it's a great liability to have a live audience," Gould told an interviewer on an album released in 1968. In emphatic sentences he was attempting to justify his decision, four years earlier, to stop performing classical music in public.

> First of all, I resent the one-timeness, the non-take-twoness, of that particular experience. As a matter of fact, I can remember many times when I did give concerts on the North American concert circuit when my performance was going rather inadequately and rather haphazardly; maybe I hadn't practised enough or I felt as if I was competing with my own

recorded version, if such exists—and I often felt that way!—and if I was, I was damned if I was going to practise for it, as a matter of fact. And if a performance were going that way, I was terribly inclined to stop—this is something that a psychiatrist would have marvellous things to say about, I'm sure—terribly inclined to stop in the middle and say, "Take two!" But one couldn't quite, without risking a scandal and very bad reviews, and so I never quite did. But I always wanted to.[2]

The interviewer prompted: Why not? Certainly it is unheard of in current concert culture, but surely an artist is entitled to stretch that culture. Gould laughed. They know they are not serious about this happening. His reply was a tease: "That would almost be worth going back and trodding the boards for, if I could really do that!" Next question.

I was nineteen in 1982, the year Glenn Gould died, and had neither met him nor heard a single one of his records—on the latter point, not least because my taste in those days ran more to the Clash and Elvis Costello than to Bach or Beethoven. Like most people, I have come to know him—if that is the right word—only through his recorded playing and his published writings. Since Gould's death, the world of music, or rather the world as it experiences music, has witnessed significant changes. Most notable of these is the ease of access to recorded music and its related consequence, the global jumbling of musical materials. Both are developments Gould would have welcomed: the first for its assumption of primacy in recorded music over performance and the second for its overturning of narratives of *musical progress,* with schools and periods succeeding one another according to a definitive account laid down by music history. What we should call the post-historical musical world—our world—is the one that Gould anticipated and advocated. At the same time, he was a self-declared puritan about art and frequently lamented music's corruption by commerce. Such are just the beginnings of his kaleidoscopic, contradictory, febrile, and brilliant mind.

Musician. Artist. Genius. Eccentric. National treasure. Celebrity. Pill-popper. Hypochondriac. Hermit. Icon. Puritan. Northerner. Joker. The story of Glenn Gould's life is one that has been told, and told well, many times and in many ways. In almost every case it has been told according to the imperatives, and fictions, of traditional biographical narrative. There is good reason to avoid doing so again.

The fiction of biography is precisely the kind of danger Gould appreciated. He was fond of play in other senses than at the keyboard, shifting personae to the point where he interviewed himself in place of traditional essays, wrote imaginary reviews under fanciful pseudonyms, and adopted costumes, characters, and accents for prolonged horsing-around sessions in the studio as well as on radio and television. His notorious retreat from performance—a move he preferred to see as a step forward into recording and disseminating true interpretations rather than tired concerts of a narrow repertoire—took him out of the public realm even as it shrouded him in an irresistible mystery. He would not make himself available except via recordings and print.

And so, lacking one Glenn Gould, the public generates multiple ones, a succession of Gould-ghosts, all of them vaporous and partial. Meanwhile, cutting across this economy of reproduction, there extends a different multiplicity, the one comprising different cultural moments. Every generation of performers after Gould has to come to terms with the lofty standards he reached. Every generation of listeners has to negotiate the implications of his advocacy of recording over performance. At the time he stopped giving concerts, the issue was alive with a McLuhanesque energy and vehemence. This may strike later observers and fans as misplaced or even absurd, but if so, it is only because Gould, ahead of his time, had already done much of the hard early thinking, the pioneering insight. In fact there can be no definitive resolution to either of these energies of multiplication and contradiction—manifold Goulds, manifold eras—and so any attempt to distill the variety of personae and interpretations into a single portrait of Glenn Gould would be false from the start, a depressing compression, as if, in the words of one writer, "a whole life could be contained by a few hundred pages—bottled, like homemade chutney."[3]

There is more to consider than just this standard objection, however, which might be levelled against any number of biographical projects. Gould's life, lived in and through music, reveals that the unified self is not just a fiction from the outside in; it is also a fiction from the inside out. The outside-in illusion underwrites the notion of a correct, or even merely convincing, interpretation of a person's life. I mean the notion of a singular self, somehow captured in the most valid representation of Gould, the one that "makes sense" of his genius as an opaque gift and of his eccentricities as the outward signs thereof. This has been attempted, and the resulting rival explanations lie before us.

The more profound, and more common, illusion is the inside-out one: the fiction that allows us to shape consciousness into a singular self in the first place, the projection of unified existence and consistent self-presentation. The two fictions, life explained as linear because assumed to be lived thus, depend upon and reinforce each other. But that also means they stand, and fall, together. Any instability experienced from the inside out gives the lie to any, and all, attempts to *explain* from the outside in. A Gould tamed into linear narrative misses the point of Gould.

Glenn Gould was well aware of the play between these illusions, and even as he sought line in music, he worked to destabilize line in life. Indeed, we may read his seeking on the one hand as a result of the felt lack on the other, a tragic awareness of contingency. Gould's stated and published ideas suggest such a philosophy of multiplicity, though nowhere does he explicitly argue the position—perhaps out of a clever intuition that enacting the instability of self would be more compelling, and certainly more amusing, than arguing it.

Thus a recurring theme in Gould's published work—work that is spiked with insights and jumbled theories—is that larger narratives of progression in music, as in life, are unreliable, even fraudulent. For example, though convinced in early professional life, typically against the grain, that a neo-traditional stance was appropriate to the modernist times, he later came to distrust sweeping stories of schools and movements, of trends and counter-trends. They were, to him, first the stuff of journalism and later, worse, the grist of music history's mill. At the same time, the unifying thought in Gould's philosophy of music—and it is primarily as a philosopher of music that I mean to treat him here—is that the single most important aspect of music is architecture, or line: the overall structure of a piece, revealed in its beauty by the act of playing. Not modulation, not timbre, not colour or tone. That is why articulation and phrasing are so central to his playing—"like an x-ray revealing a skeleton," he said; it is also why the complexity of structure combined with the freedom of interpretation of J.S. Bach's expansive oeuvre drew him so often, and so movingly. Though he resisted the label of "Bach specialist," Gould played Bach and other masters of fugue and counterpoint more frequently than the music of the thirty-odd canonical figures whose works he recorded.

This love of line was also what made him say that playing the Tudor master William Byrd gave him "great delight" or that, on at least three separate recorded occasions, his "favourite composer" was Orlando Gibbons—"certainly the composer with whom, at some mysterious spiritual level I won't begin to explain, I most identify." Asked in 1970 by *High Fidelity* to list his "desert island discs," Gould mentioned as first choice a Deller Consort recording of

Gibbons's hymns and anthems "because ever since my teen-age years this music (and for close to fifteen years this particular record by the Deller Consort) has moved me more deeply than any other sound experience I can think of. In fact, this is the only disc in my collection three copies of which I have literally worn out."[4]

These late-Elizabethan composers wrote few pieces for keyboard, and Gould recorded only one disc that features them—sadly, since his playing on this record is among his best, intellectual and moving in equal measure. Indeed, his engagement with Gibbons and Byrd may be easily dismissed as a footnote to his lengthy performance-based arguments with Mozart and Beethoven, two composers he claimed to dislike, or his extended meditation on Bach's contrapuntal genius. But Gibbons and Byrd—"the two northern masters," he called them, a term of high praise for this lover of northern climes and their chilly solitudes—offer purity of composition, a structure almost mathematical in its elegance, even as they presage large changes in music's orientation. As Gould put it, what we have here is "a reminder of those antecedents of the modern world which one could endeavour to extenuate in quite a different fashion than post-Renaissance tradition decreed."[5]

Gould followed the trail of an apparently stray, single B-flat note in Byrd's "Sellinger's Round"—a sign of something new in Tudor music, he argued, the harbinger of the modern developments to come. He suggested that the two Tudor composers "share an idiom but not an attitude," with Gibbons standing as the lugubrious Gustav Mahler to Byrd's exuberant Richard Strauss. Taken together, they reveal the line of beauty that made Gould love music, the love that made him a musician. Byrd and Gibbons also, as *fin de siècle* composers, occupy a moment of transition—something Gould clearly relished in them and in his own late-millennial circumstances. In their case, it was toward "that new key-oriented chord system to which, within a few years, most music would subscribe." What we take for granted, a conventional set of keys and chords, these two minor geniuses anticipated. What did Gould anticipate in his own transitional moment, which we may now, or soon, take for granted? I will endeavour to answer that question in this book.

We tread on uneven ground, however. Both music history and music are typically structured as forms of what we might call *experienced consequence*. They offer tales of temporal succession explained according to claims of causal succession. However useful or even necessary, such narratives are illusory. They construct, over the negotiation of actual moments in time, an arc of larger meaning that could not have been available in the moments themselves, that is superimposed.[6] Biography, too, is a form of illusory consequence. That is why I have decided to tell Gould's story—really a linked set of ideas about perception, consciousness, time, and silence—not as a story but as a single contested piece considered from a variety of angles.

François Girard's 1993 work, *Thirty Two Short Films About Glenn Gould,* revealed the pianist from a variety of angles. Why thirty-two? Devotees of Gould's recorded works know the answer immediately. In Bach's *Goldberg Variations,*[7] the work allegedly composed as an insomnia cure for Dresden's Count Von Keyserlingk, to be played by his court harpsichordist Johann Gottlieb Goldberg, the variations consist of a tonally and rhythmically linked series of thirty variations on the thirty-two-bar aria announced at the beginning. The aria itself, possibly written for Bach's wife, dates from 1725 and is repeated da capo as the final element of the piece. Not only is the overall work a superbly realized exercise in theme-and-variation composition, it was and remains one of the most devilishly difficult pieces ever composed for keyboard.

The thirty variations range from subtle trills to elaborate deconstructions of the theme, arranged in nine interlocked canons. The progressive variation of ground bass, rather than soprano melody, makes it an example of *ruggiero*, akin to the chaconne or passacaglia forms that Bach also created but with irregular inversions along the way—thus "a passacaglia worked out in chiaroscuro," as Albert Schweitzer said. With the initial aria reprised as a coda, we have thirty-two works within the work: theme and variation and theme again. It is, Gould himself wrote, "the most brilliant substantiation of ground bass in history."[8] (The film's thirty-two short sections do not exactly mimic the structure of the *Variations*; it is nevertheless an excellent example of fractured biography.)

Famously, Gould recorded the *Variations* twice. The first was in 1955, at Columbia's 30th Street studios between June 10 and 16; the disc was released to immediate wide acclaim, cementing his already growing performance reputation. The second was in 1981, during April and May, just before the same studios were slated for demolition and just a year before his death at the age of fifty. The two versions have been much compared. Perhaps the simplest way to articulate the difference between them is that the 1955 version is the work of a young man, the 1981 that of a mature one. The first is arrogant, almost callow, with bravura displays of speed and chilly dexterity and an overall tone that is brilliant but somewhat uninflected. The second, recorded because

Gould said he wanted to try again to find line in the work, is slower, warmer, almost elegiac; the ground-bass unity emerges more clearly, as do the rubato and dynamic-range possibilities of the piano. Here the trademark humming of the player, clearly audible even on inferior playback equipment, offers a kind of harmonic counterpoint to the sound of the piano's struck keys, man and instrument conjoined in performance.

Or so, in retrospect, we might be tempted to see things. Which of these recordings one prefers is a matter of taste, or temperament, or age. Sometimes it is a matter of the time of day.

In 1955, labouring in the first of countless experiences in the recording studio, Gould struggled with the piece—not the technical details but, as so often later, with creating a version of the whole that matched his inner sense of the music's logic. The engineers at Columbia's studios in New York—who later would tell sometimes exaggerated tales of the young Canadian's evident eccentricities, his pre-recital ritual handsoaks in ice water, the peculiar hunched posture and proclivity for Polar mineral water and arrowroot biscuits—were at once impressed and frustrated by his perfectionism. This stubbornness in the studio would become a defining, to some degree a destroying, feature of Gould's life. And the eccentricities would be co-opted immediately as publicity fodder: a June 25 press release from Columbia archly summarized the "rituals, foibles or fancies" of its young star, including the bottles of pills and twenty minutes of cold soaking. Also the collapsible chair, described as "the Goldberg (Rube) variation of them all," with its four adjustable legs: "The studio skeptics thought this was wackiness of the highest order until recording got under way. Then they saw Glenn adjust the slant of his chair before doing his slightly incredible cross-hand passages in the Variations."[9]

In the liner notes for the record, Gould's earliest significant publication, he offered the following brilliant if somewhat earnest assessment:

> We have observed, by means of a technical dissection, that the aria is incompatible with its offspring, that the crucial bass by its very perfection of outline and harmonic implications stunts its own growth and prohibits the accustomed passacaglia evolution towards a cumulative point. We have observed, also by analysis, that the aria's thematic content reveals an equally exclusive disposition, that the motivic elaboration in each variation is a law unto itself, and that, by consequence, there are no plateaus of successive variation using similar principles in design such as

lend architectural coherence to the variations of Beethoven and Brahms. Yet without analysis we have sensed that there exists a fundamental coordinating intelligence which we labeled "ego." Thus we are forced to revise our criteria, which were scarcely designed to arbitrate the union of music and metaphysics—the realm of technical transcendence.[10]

Gould would produce numerous personal manifestos and *ars poetica* summaries in later life. Indeed, the manifesto is high among his favourite literary forms, just as it was for the Evelyn Waugh character in *Put Out More Flags* who, we are told, "had always rather specialized in manifestos. He had written one at school; he had written a dozen at the University; once, in the late twenties, he and his friends Hat and Malpractice had even issued the invitation to a party in the form of a manifesto. It was one of his many reasons for shunning communism that its manifesto had been written for it, once and for all, by somebody else." Gould never entirely outgrew the particular temptation for the young man, especially of intellectual inclination, to state his personal beliefs as a way of setting the world straight. The paragraph above, though characteristically difficult to follow, remains the clearest expression of his self-conception as a musician, and especially as an interpreter of Bach. Somewhere in the tension between the analytic desire for architectural coherence and the non-analytic awareness of an underlying singular intelligence lies the secret to his life as a performer and artist.

The haunting *Goldberg* aria, not the most technically difficult section of the work, proved intractable. Having delivered masterly versions of the sections demanding tricky crossovers and transitions, Gould could not get it right. He and the engineers recorded it twenty times without avail. On the twenty-first take, Gould was satisfied. "It was a question," he said later, "of utilizing the first twenty takes to erase all superfluous expressions from my reading of it, and there is nothing more difficult to do."[11] The aria you hear when you play that disc is quintessential Gould: the technical assurance, hinting at the astonishing virtuosity to come, announcing an interpretation of almost clinical precision. But although it comes first on the recording, and is forever the single audible version of this section of this recording, there are in fact twenty-one renderings of the same piece of music. One is the chosen version, the official story. It could not be such without the other twenty. Where, or how, do they exist?

Not thirty-two variations then, but twenty-one takes: same score, different interpretations, seeking the acceptable one, the one to be released as well as recorded.

Other biographies have tried to explain Gould's personal eccentricities in terms of his music, or vice versa. Whatever the conclusion, they are all bound to a standard presumption of biography, that it has to make unified sense of its subject, to find a single narrative line through the life. But life, as Gould well knew, does not follow such linear progression, and even as he was devoted to line in musical compositions, he was hostile to the idea of progressive, sense-conferring narratives.

I take that hostility seriously in thinking about Gould's life and work. There is no unifying theme, no resolution to the tonic, in his life. His ideas about music govern that life, but those ideas themselves are contradictory, paradoxical, mischievous, and deliberately provocative. In fashioning a philosophical biography, I have abandoned standard narrative form and instead adopted a kaleidoscopic frame. Each of my takes is a version of Gould, always partial, always unfinished. Played over and over, always slightly different, always in search of aptness and insight, Gould is here the subject of a sort of bio-philosophical recording session.[12]

CHAPTER TWO

Silence

Music arises from silence and subsides into silence. Silence is woven through music, in the space between the notes, without which the notes could not exist. Music seeks and flees silence in the same moment. Thus, indeed, are moments created: the negotiation of the present as it pushes into the future, finding its line. Not all silence is the same, and not just because of duration or placement. "Silence too can be plagiarized," a music critic reminds us.[13]

Life arises from non-existence and subsides into death. It is sustained in time by its own suspension. An ancient image of this span: a bird flies through a feasting hall, from one end to the other. Entry, fleeting presence, and then exit. Consciousness is created in memory's uneasy, inescapable conjunction with the nothingness on either side of our lives. What is the silence between the notes? What is the person before or after his death?

Bare life is not the self. The self is as much burden as achievement, a constant weight of expectation and responsibility that we lug through life, the time of life. The self can be an accuser, a betrayer, a wayward child. The gap we feel in that humping weight is the distance between me as I live and myself as implicated by the other—the one who sees me, who judges me. The weight is also, however, an awareness of a different gap, the one between me as I live and the fact of being itself, the sheer inarticulable being-here of existing.[14] Call this the self-alienation effect. Awareness of this existential alienation may be the beginning of shame, of responsibility, of despair. Perhaps of all three at once.

Everyone is subject to this awareness: it is the price of selfhood. We are all performers, having to drag out the self-character for one more show, one more gig, day after day. And if one is a performer, a player, in more than the shared existential sense . . .

Glenn Herbert Gould was born on September 25, 1932, the only child of Russell Herbert "Bert" Gould and Florence Emma Gould (née Grieg—she was a distant cousin of Norwegian composer Edvard Grieg). Glenn's parents were both musical, though not professionally, playing and singing in church and social groups. By trade Bert was a salesman for the family fur business, Gold Standard Furs. They lived at 32 Southwood Drive in Toronto's Beach neighbourhood, then a largely white-bread Anglo-Protestant enclave at some distance from the city's core, especially isolated in winter when its long lakefront can be bleak, the visible water wide as an ocean.

They also had a cottage north of Toronto on Lake Simcoe, a source of great consolation—and welcome solitude—at all times of Gould's life. In his middle age, the cottage was a cherished haven, often in winter when the summer tourist population had given way to the dedicated loners. In early life, matters were more complicated. Unlike his father, an avid fly fisherman, Glenn did not take to angling as one of his favoured modes of silence. In the summer of 1939, aged six, he caught his first and only fish while out with a neighbour and his children. "I suddenly saw this thing entirely from the fish's point of view," he recalled later, and in his distress went into a boat-rocking tantrum that ruined the outing and alienated him from the other children. "I immediately went to work on my father to convince him he should abandon fishing. It took me ten years, but this is probably the greatest thing I have ever done." In later years he was even more proactive, roaring around the lake in his boat, dressed in overcoat and cap, to disrupt the summer bass and perch hunters of southern Ontario.[15]

Gould entered Williamson Road Public School in grade two after private tutoring. School bored him, and he was the subject of bullying both real and imagined. He skipped grade three. At age five he announced he was destined to be a great composer. East-end Toronto contemporaries recall a bright and already eccentric child who had a keen sense of his own impressive future. Later Gould attended Malvern Collegiate Institute, where he was a good, if not spectacular, student; he did not graduate because he refused to take the mandatory physical education examination. He studied music at the Toronto (now Royal) Conservatory of Music, including nine years with teacher Alberto Guerrero. He would later claim to be self-taught and did not take on students of his own.

His life was spent performing, first in public as well as in the studio, later in the studio alone. He never married, though he had at least one substantial relationship, albeit with a married woman, between 1967 and 1971. She moved to Toronto with her two children, lived close to Gould, but eventually returned to her husband. Gould asked her to marry him, but she refused, and then he called her every night for two years after the affair had ended. She finally persuaded him to stop calling, and they never saw each other again.

Glenn Gould died on October 4, 1982, just days after his fiftieth birthday. Acquaintances say he had predicted this half-century death. It is clear that, in more than one way, he precipitated it.

Beginning, end.

CHAPTER THREE

Fiction

Personhood is a function of memory; it is also a fiction of memory. We cannot be ourselves if we cannot recall our past to our conscious minds each waking morning. Memory is fractured and hazy, distorted and untrustworthy; but it is all we have. Destroy memory and our strandedness in time is complete, our sense of duration and passage obliterated. Now we lose ourselves in timelessness. That, surely, describes the non-experience or absence of consciousness we call death.

Paradoxically, we seek this same timelessness in life: moments of self's annulment or transcendence, instants of self-loss. These are not really moments or instants, to be sure. They have no experienced temporal measure. They are times out of time, marking our lives as surely as life's beginning and end.

Theme and variation, expectation and resolution. Music reveals its architecture by existing in time. We sense a building movement, a problem is somehow announced. Our minds, attuned to the ways of music, frame and anticipate the possible outcomes. In this manner, music makes us feel our way forward into the future before that future has arrived. When it does arrive—when anticipated future becomes experienced present—the past is resolved into sense, into something like (but not *exactly* like) meaning. Music's time is a time of conversion: it makes succession into progression. The silence at the end of the piece, always anticipated and then experienced, works like the end of a poem or the white space at the conclusion of a book. There could be no music, no poem, no book without that which underscores it, the line drawn at the end, the nothingness to come. Thus is sense delivered, via time, as the experience of consequence—as if caused, as if inevitable.

I suggested that biography, like history, is a consequential narrative. Traditionally, it sets itself a simple-sounding but difficult task. It seeks to resolve the contingency of person-hood, one's strandedness in time, precisely by converting succession into progression—what that master of narratology, Paul Ricoeur, called the *emplotment* of self in a unified narrative.[16] A biography says: here is why this single person became this singular artist. (Or statesman, or philosopher.) Without being fictional, it remains a fiction. Consider the general problem of progression, found alike in music, stories, and persons.

"The experience of a linear 'organic' flow of events is an illusion (albeit a necessary one)," says Slavoj Žižek. The illusion masks the fact that consistency, and so meaning, is only achieved retroactively, from the standpoint of the ending. Indeed, that is what an ending is, the point at which I can turn around and mask the "radical contingency" of my narrative in the very act of imposing it on contingent events, moments that all might have been otherwise. "But if this illusion is a result of the very linearity of the narration," Žižek wonders, "how can the radical contingency of the enchainment of events be made visible? The answer is perhaps obvious: precisely by proceeding in a reverse way, by presenting the events backward, from the end to the beginning."[17]

Such illuminating reverse counterexamples can only be found in time-based media, where we can in fact run the story backwards: such films as Harold Pinter's *Betrayal* (1982) or Christopher Nolan's *Memento* (2000). Even here, the discrete chunks of narrative, however fractured and rearranged, still must be "run" forward. (An exception is the short opening and closing sequences of *Memento,* run in slow-motion reverse.) Shifting end and beginning emphasizes the power of narrative expectation; it does not actually challenge it.

The basic impulse of narrative is sequence: this happened, and then this happened. In *bare narrative,* the sort offered by children or bores, the sequencing lacks consequence and is reduced to mere stated succession: and then, and then, and then. The felt lack in such a tale illustrates E.M. Forster's famous difference between story and plot: the queen died and then the king died is a *story;* the queen died and then the king died of grief is a *plot.* In *adorned narrative,* or plot, there must be some demonstrated enchainment of events, the creation of consequence. Only under these conditions is it possible to experience the libidinal release promised by all narrative, the sense of the *fitting end.*

The narrative presupposes the very thing it means to find, namely meaning under the sign of consequential structure: not just *and then, and then* but also *and then, therefore, and thus; and thus, therefore, and then.*

Consider the comparison to music. One may record the notations that indicate music, just as one may record the symbols that encode a narrative or an argument. But the logic of music's consequence cannot be exhibited except in the playing. The complex structure of the *Brandenburg Concertos* is available all at once as the score of the piece, but it is fully present only in the temporal experience of hearing the notes in time, pattern and meta-pattern unfolded between one silence and another. And then *therefore* and thus. And thus *therefore* and then. The story proceeds. The argument runs.

The piece resolves in the hearing, it plays, but the background tension does not go away. Is this experience of structure inherent in the piece or in our desire for the piece to mean, for the story to make sense?

Can it be any wonder that Gould's life, increasingly reclusive and eccentric, resists easy resolution? Or that it has proved the stuff of actual fiction? Thomas Bernhard's novel *The Loser* is the best of these, an extended interior monologue, in one continuous paragraph, by a man who had studied music with Gould and been obliterated by the shadow that genius casts over talent.[18] Another friend and fellow student, Wertheimer, has committed suicide under the pressure of Gould's extraordinary example—or, more precisely, by the fictional Gould's uttering the word *loser* (*Untergeher*) to him, "in his straightforward Canadian-American way," even as Wertheimer recalled hearing Gould tackle the *Goldberg Variations* in a manner that definitively proved the difference between genius and talent. "They were originally composed *to delight the soul* and almost two hundred and fifty years later they have killed a hopeless person. . . . Wertheimer's fate was to have walked past room thirty-three in the Mozarteum at the precise moment when Glenn Gould was playing the so-called *aria* in that room."[19]

The narrator has, instead of killing himself, turned to philosophy—suicide on the instalment plan.[20] "I will now devote myself to philosophical matters, I thought as I walked to my teacher's house, even though of course I didn't have the faintest idea what these philosophical matters might be." One of these is what he calls his "Glenn Essay"—a work that is forever being contemplated, attempted, and destroyed because it is imperfect, its categories expanding beyond limit: "*Glenn and ruthlessness, Glenn and solitude, Glenn and Bach, Glenn and the Goldberg Variations,* I thought. *Glenn in his studio in the woods, his hatred of people, his hatred of music, his music-people hatred,* I thought. *Glenn and simplicity,* I thought . . . "[21]

Is the present book an attempt at the Glenn Essay? Impossible to say. But, simple fact: the central mystery remains. What is the valid interpretation, the good story, to tell about a life, especially a life lived in music? How to create anticipation and resolution?

Perhaps as the music they are.

CHAPTER FOUR

Memory

Where, and how, does a person exist?

The neurologist Oliver Sacks relates the following terrifying case: in 1985, Clive Wearing, an English musician, musicologist, and conductor in his mid-forties, was struck by a ravaging brain infection, herpes encephalitis, which destroyed most of the brain matter governing memory.[22] Like the character played by Guy Pearce in *Memento,* Wearing was left in a state of consciousness where his memory lasted only a few seconds. (Actually, that's considerably worse than Pearce's vengeful Leonard, who can remember for minutes at a time and track his murder plot by means of *aide-memoire* tattoos applied to his body.)

Wearing's condition, a kind of living death, is so hard to imagine that Sacks spends considerable time furnishing details. The musician repeatedly greets friends during a short visit, as if they have returned from lengthy absences. He can move around his apartment but, if asked, cannot say where anything is. He can carry on a conversation, after a fashion, but only by stringing together familiar themes and non sequiturs. The one person he recognizes reliably is his wife, Deborah.

This, let it be said, is the functional Wearing. For years after his illness he was despondent, a suicidal man without the capacity to plan, let alone execute, his own suicide. His journal from this period consists of entries, made every few minutes and then crossed out, that read: "2:10 pm: this time properly awake . . . 2:14 pm: this time finally awake . . . 2:35 pm: this time completely awake." Later: "At 9:40 pm I awoke for the first time, despite my previous claims."[23] Not even the gods who punished Sisyphus could have conceived a more devilish sentence.

But then: music. Wearing no longer remembers anything about the composers he wrote about, nor can he name pieces when they are played to him; but he can still play and can even conduct. Arising from silence, music is his sole refuge, memory or no memory. Representing nothing, as composer Arnold Schoenberg asserted, music creates anticipation, expectation, promise, and resolution. We call music a *time-based medium,* but it is perhaps more accurate to say that time is a *music-revealed condition.*

Clive Wearing would not remember this sentence by the time you finish reading it. Only music retains the power to cradle and wrap him in its measured moments. Sacks quotes T.S. Eliot's *Four Quartets:* "You are the music / while the music lasts."

Reflect for a moment on the relation among memory, mind, and identity. The standard story goes this way: I am only able to be myself if I can remember, from moment to moment and day to day, the story of my self. The narrative of singularity. Remove that and I am not I; I am not at all. But memory is a complex property, and not just because it can be broken into short-term, long-term, and contextual. The last is most persistent: Clive Wearing could remember that Margaret Thatcher was prime minister—though actually she no longer was—when he could not remember whom he was talking to from moment to moment. Memory is not all in the mind, however; or rather, more precisely, mind is not all in the head.

Inga and Otto are going to a museum. Inga, in good health, has memorized the directions to get her there. Otto, suffering from memory loss, has written down the directions because he knows he will forget. What is the difference? We want to say that Inga knows how to get there while Otto does not because he has forgotten. But are written directions not in a sense an extension of Otto's mind, functionally identical to Inga's memory? She, after all, consults her memory just as Otto does his notes; indeed, in way-finding, many people rely on what is known as eidetic, or image-based, memory. That is, Inga may well call up in her mind a visual image of the map she consulted before leaving home. Otto's notes are part of his mind, even though they exist physically apart from his brain. He and his notes are part of a coupled system that is cognitive in its own right.[24]

Gould had a prodigious memory for music, possibly the most highly developed memory of his generation. It is impossible now to know just how his memory worked for him, but some generalizations can be hazarded.

Musicians rarely, if ever, employ eidetic memory to play music: that is to say, even if they learned a piece from its score rather than aurally, they do not conjure up an image of the notes scored on bars in order to play. Musical memory is more organic: it depends on felt structure, so that progressions in notes can be executed smoothly, correctly. A piece can only be remembered *in the playing*, not all at once. Players who sight-read from scores are thus engaged in a complex cognitive feedback pattern, whereby their eye-mind is processing information one way even as their finger-mind is producing results in a structurally different manner. Part of the joy we take in great performance is cognitive, something well beyond our admiration, however real, for mere dexterity in fingering or sureness in attack and release. Playing a piano, whether from memory or before a score, is an enacted demonstration of the mind's power, extended in space and across time.

No mind is unextended. The score serves to render the composition, to fix it in place when it can no longer be held merely in mind. Also to communicate it to others. The same can be said of a recording. Tape and disc are extensions of mind just as paper is—that is why the mind of Glenn Gould is still accessible to us; it is *on the record*. At the margins of complexity and innovation, we are all Ottos rather than Ingas: we need tools of notation and arrangement to keep our minds in function. What else is writing except the most ancient and powerful of these tools? Except it is a tool that uses us as much as we use it. Or more precisely, it *is* us. We speak of these storage devices as *media*, to signify their position between source and target of meaning, their vehicular status shunting words or music or images from place to place. In fact there is no between because there is no distance, only extension. The medium is the mind.

The mind is also the medium. We speak of memorized lyrics or songs as *known by heart*. The ancient Greeks seated cognition in the largest and most important of the internal organs—courage and identity belonged to the liver, that sustaining organ, and so that is where the gods centred their punishment of Prometheus for the crime of stealing fire, his eaten daily by Zeus's eagle, only to grow back for further torture. Later the seat of selfhood would move northeast, from the liver to the heart, where it has remained for centuries. We still speak of "eating our hearts out," and we approve the things that only the heart knows, the reasons it has that reason alone cannot understand, though now we usually mean things about love. And to know things *by heart* means to *record* them, from the Latin *recordari,* from *re* and *cordis*—heart. Rendered on the heart, in other words, stored there, a sweet cordial for the mind. What else?

Gould, like Marshall McLuhan, understood this, just as he must also have appreciated McLuhan's argument that the world was shifting, almost before their mid-century eyes, from the modern dominance of visual space, with its culture of print and reason and record, to a postmodern moment ruled by acoustic space and its electronic penchant for emotion and visual stimulation. The two men did not see eye to eye on many things, as two such towering egos could not be expected to, but they both appreciated the importance of mind extension even as they worked out, in their different ways, a philosophy of communication and the acoustic. At a time when their shared home, Toronto, was vibrant with deep thought about technology and culture—the time and place of Harold Innis and Northrop Frye, also the conservative shadow of George Grant, as well as themselves—they dug deep into the strange fact of consciousness and the way technology, even an elderly form of it such as the keyboard, can reveal us to ourselves.

Neither Gould nor McLuhan was able to appreciate the full force of the insight, however. McLuhan's notion of media as "extensions of man" gets much right about the nature of the extension, the desire for it, and its various instruments, with their bright promises and dark secrets; but it does not probe deeply enough into the mysteries of mind that man, or woman, is blessed with.[25] Gould, meanwhile, was not rigorous in pursuing his initial, striking insight and so ran into confusions. Like many gifted musicians, he would sometime speak of the music he heard "inside his head" and was given to defending his notorious humming at the keyboard as an uncontrolled echo of that inner music. But the concept of inwardness is misplaced here; it is a misunderstanding of his own memory. Memory is not the vast aviary imagined in Plato's *Theaetetus,* a storehouse of flitting birds we try, with limited success, to catch in hand. Memory, like mind more generally, is the embodiment of a person negotiating a world. Creating a world, indeed; and finding out, in so doing, who else is listening.

CHAPTER FIVE

Existence

But then: where, or how, does music exist?

Is music the notes as they are arranged on the score, that is, the physical document? Surely not. By analogy, we would have to say that a book is just its physical manifestation as type upon a page. Do we want to say that?

Is this music?

Is music the sum total of its performances and recordings, the always-in-progress lifetime of a piece as it moves from gestation to debut to interpretation and perhaps canonization? This sounds more convincing.

And yet, any brute summing of performances, though it might appear to free the piece from its mere embodiment on the page, breaking the shackles of matter and re-investing music in time, seems by the same token to make it a prisoner of temporality. At the very least, in this view a piece of music can never be finished, its essence forever deferred.

Is music, then, something else altogether? A transcendental reality, perhaps, sustained beyond mere performance or material, rendering these the simple vehicles or reflections of true music? In this view, music might be something like the Platonic Forms or, better, the sound of the celestial spheres as they slowly perform their eternal, harmonious, cosmic dance. What we hear on this mortal plane, the mundane passing of air past a reed to cause vibration, a bow of sheep's hair passed over a piece of catgut, a taut string deftly plucked or struck with a hammer, are only pale shadows of the divine chords. At best, they are capable merely of hinting at the beauties in a realm beyond human hearing.

Or is music more like language, where meaning is captured by the play of sameness and difference? We hear the same note now and later, when it does not perform the same function or take on the same significance. We see the same letter in this word and that, we hear the same word here and there. Meaning, in music or in language, is never reducible to any single element of its enactment. It is, instead, an emergent property of the structures of iteration and reiteration, performance and repetition.

That sounds fine, except that, though we sometimes speak of the language of music, and music meets language at more than one juncture—poetry, chorale—music itself does not seem to mean the way language does. Its singularity is more resistant, and its significance more pliable. The novelist and poet Nancy Huston: "Meaning is hard as a rock, but music is porous like soapstone."[26] Music seems to be non-parseable, not to be translated or otherwise rendered. Indeed, it does not seem to *mean* at all. (Perhaps a poem does not either? Archibald MacLeish thought so.)[27]

Is music perhaps none of these philosophical fictions, these conceptual chimerae, at all? Is it rather a feature of complex brain function, like the relations of mathematics or the sense of viable composition? What we recognize as the beauty of the piece is analogous to the perceived elegance of a logical deduction: the demonstrated truth of Occam's Razor in action, as we reach the conclusion in fewer steps or retain identical functionality using a smaller number of moving parts. Music has structure. We might even say it *is* structure, audibly revealed. Our conscious minds, themselves structured to recognize structure, respond to music as a hungry man does to food. The rich pleasure we experience at perceiving music's play of pattern—theme and variation, anticipation and resolution—is what we mean when we say we are moved by music.

Or is music a social and cultural phenomenon, like the rituals and religions with which it is so often associated? Seen this way, music is an elaborate semiotic system, a network of human communications grids. It thus has the ability to exhibit a wide range of functions that we class under the contested notion of *human nature*. As neuroscientist/musician Daniel Levitin has categorized it, for example, music can do some or all of the following: facilitate friendship, excite joy, convey knowledge, provide comfort, bolster religion, and communicate love.[28]

All true. And yet what does that tell us about *music*? The emphasis is a mark of frustration, the special italics of impasse. The more we seek to define music, the more it evades us. We know it when we hear it, to be sure. Increasingly, we can hear it anytime and anywhere, for, unlike in previous eras, music is now comprehensively available. So much so, indeed, that its rarity in daily experience—once the chief feature of music's presence in cultural and individual life—is now almost as unimaginable as a world without internal combustion or running water. But what do we think we know when we know *that*?

It is a fallacy to assume even that love of music is universal. Kingsley Amis's Lucky Jim Dixon is surely the exception when he complains about being subjected to "some skein of untiring facetiousness by filthy Mozart" and then "some Brahms rubbish," followed by "a violin sonata by some Teutonic bore." Unlucky him, we might think, at least for the Mozart. But that *some* is indicative: these are curses, not philistinism. Dixon takes the canonical names in vain as a way of letting out his particular *cri de coeur,* that of a man who spends his life being bored by other people, especially his employers.

But what about Vladimir Nabokov? In *Speak, Memory* he wrote that music sounded to him "merely as an arbitrary succession of more or less irritating sounds. . . . The concert piano and all wind instruments bore me in small doses and flay me in larger ones." Sigmund Freud professed himself a fan of art but found music without pleasure because some "turn of mind in me rebels against being moved by a thing without knowing why I am thus affected and what it is that affects me."

Most of us are not so afflicted, or so resistant. Love of music is universal across all human cultures—though not without considerable variation—and the large majority of us enjoy it daily, usually deeply and without question. The ancient Greeks thought music was celestial and eternal, like mathematics. Modern cognitive science suggests it answers our "appetite for gratuitous difficulty." Teenagers everywhere know that music is identity in its easiest form, invidious distinction based on taste.

As Gould ardently wished, music is now easier to get than ever, easier to have with us at every moment, not any music but *all* music, the iPod-fed soundtracking of every-day life the logical outcome of our deep animal pleasure in the aural. Almost inconceivable now to recall how we used to have to take a bus across the city to visit the guy who had sub-woofers and a good record collection, sitting around the basement rec room to listen to *London Calling* or *Armed Forces,* or the way mix tapes were passed around like secret tokens of cool in an era before nearly instanta-neous MP3 downloads.[29] And how much more bizarre those scenes in *The Magic Mountain,* where a gramophone and a stack of records utterly transform life in Thomas Mann's alpine sanatorium?

Purists complain still, as they did when Gould was among the first to advocate recording techniques over performance, that ubiquity of music lessens our regard for it, but there is no evidence of this. Hans Castorp plays a recording of Schubert's "Linden-tree" over and over, his love renewed timelessly each time. But the implications go further than this. Musical taste has for centuries been structured by the matrix of technological availability. Music could be enjoyed only by those who could afford to create it, and those with less pressing relations to the conditions of necessity could afford to create it *complexly*. Thus the emergence of *legitimate* musical taste around the *classical* music of formal experimentation found in the European religious and court traditions. Music moves from its homes in liturgy and dance to become an aesthetic end in itself, an art form. And increasingly it is subject to the claims of Kantian disinterestedness—that it should be appreciated for other purposes than the inherent beauty it delivers.

But that idea of anti-utilitarian, or pure, aesthetic enjoyment is itself revealed as a class property rather than a fundamental quality of mind. It establishes the *taste* position of those rare (usually wealthy) few who can afford to experience music in this fashion. Any taste system based on rarity grows unstable when material conditions alter, especially when there are changes in the basic distribution of availability. The formal concert evening to which Gould would object is, from this viewpoint, merely the last morbid excrescence of an aristocratic system of taste. Falsely democratic, apparently open to anyone's enjoyment, it is still governed by the lexical values of *good taste* in music. Moreover, his refusal can be seen as marking the classical concert's perverse zombie energy, its dying spasm. As a form of canonical taste becomes endangered by real democratization—for example, that of popular music disseminated by radio and recording—the more energetically and desperately it tries to assert its authority.[30]

CHAPTER SIX

Genius

We look for the signs of genius to explain what we cannot otherwise explain. "There was never a genius without a tincture of madness," Aristotle said, and even a scientific world retains a peculiar faith in the idea that genius is a divine gift, a visitation. *Inspiration* means to breathe into, and even now, in a more secular and less mysterious age, we may feel that a special air belongs to those who can do something we cannot imagine doing, something high-percentile and rare.

The romantic narrative of genius works to nudge divine madness, otherworldly and mysterious, into a natural and less explosive category. Genius shall be evident from the earliest moments—or at least the *post facto* back-story will make it so. Mozart's childhood compositions are unarguable, as are the sketches of Picasso. In Gould's case, we grasp at slighter evidence: his father reported that the young Gould would hum rather than cry and would, reaching up his arms, "flex his fingers almost as if playing a scale." More reliably, from the age of three Gould showed evidence of perfect pitch, identifying tonality and modulation with assurance—a necessary condition for the vast musical memory he would later exhibit, surely a cornerstone, if not in fact the crucial conduit, for his sense of self, his reliable personhood.

It has to be conceded that pitch is no guarantee of an ability to compose, let alone compose well. Pitch is neither sufficient nor strictly necessary for musical creation. Though Gould was making up his own tunes by age five, including some that were performed at his school or in church, and meanwhile showed great accuracy and precision at the keyboard, singing the notes as he played them, his own efforts at mature composition are indifferent at best. His one success-ful recorded work, String Quartet op. 1, was an attempt at counterpoint in which, as he himself admitted, he made all the rookie mistakes of the composer's game. It was also composed in a classical style that, in the year of its origin (1953), any ardent advocate of twelve-tone avant-gardism such as Gould should have abhorred.

He liked to insist, instead, that his compositions in "contrapuntal radio" showed his real compositional talent—not least his documentary "The Idea of North" (1967) and, as a small but telling example, his charming 1963 creation called "So You Want to Write a Fugue"—a multi-voice layering of advice for prospective composers of counterpoint, first broadcast on CBC-TV as the finale to a program entitled *The Art of the Fugue* and later released by Columbia on the two-disc *Glenn Gould Silver Jubilee Album* (1980): "So you want to write a fugue? You've got the urge to write a fugue? You've got the nerve to write a fugue? The only way to write one is to plunge right in and write one. But never be clever for the sake of being clever, for the sake of showing off!"[31]

At the same time, Gould would often agree to, sometimes even favour, the phrase *recreative* (rather than *creative*) artist for his own musical interventions at the keyboard. Every interpretation is a new work in its own right, something especially true of the Bach oeuvre, whose lack of specified tempi or phrasing leave decisions about pacing, articulation, and ornamentation largely in the hands of its player or conductor. Though one works in the vertical dimension of the stave, herding the motive along as it performs the business of progression from moment to moment, one can only do so with a keen awareness of the horizontal dimension of the work, its architecture—another issue for interpretation. Add to this the dynamic and colour possibilities available to the pianist, unknown to the composer working on clavichord or harpsichord, and it is easy to see that there is indeed such a thing as a genius of interpretation.

On January 3, 1964, *Time* magazine, that arbiter of mainstream legitimacy, proclaimed the thirty-one-year-old Gould's recording career "little short of genius." He had yet to record even half of what he would eventually produce in the studio, including many of his now most-prized albums.

All that lay far in the future. His parents later insisted they did not want Gould to have the skewed life of a musical freak—the words *Mozart* and *prodigy* were banned from the household lexicon—but from the start his mother was convinced that he would be a supremely gifted musician, in particular as a concert pianist. Music was everywhere in his life from a point before birth: anticipating a later fad, during pregnancy Gould's mother played music often to stimulate fetal development.

Gould's first public performance came on June 5, 1938, at age five: he accompanied his parents' vocal duet at the thirtieth-anniversary celebration of the Business Men's Bible Class, of which his father was a member. In August of the same year he was a contestant in a piano competition held at the Canadian National Exhibition but did not win. On December 9, his second public performance was at the Emmanuel Presbyterian Church in Toronto. His playing astonished the audience, and young Glenn began saying he wanted to be a concert pianist.

By 1944 Gould was competing in Kiwanis Music Festivals, an experience he would later discuss with derision. Winning a $200 prize in the first of these also brought his first press coverage. He was twelve. The next year, on December 12, 1945, he made his professional organ debut, graduating from churches and provincial competitions to the Eaton Auditorium in downtown Toronto. He played Mendelssohn's Sonata no. 6, the Concerto Movement by Dupuis, and the Fugue in F Major by J.S. Bach. A review in the Toronto *Evening Telegram* called him a genius—the first public application of the magic word.

On May 8, 1946, he played for the first time with an orchestra, performing the first movement of Beethoven's Concerto no. 4 with the Toronto Conservatory Symphony at Massey Hall. The critics were respectful. On January 14 and 15, 1947, he made his professional debut with the Toronto Symphony Orchestra, performing all four movements of Beethoven's Concerto no. 4. Critics noted his distracting onstage fidgets, later explained as the result of allergenic dog hair on his suit.

Really? On October 20 of the same year Gould gave his first full recital in the Eaton Auditorium's "International Artists" series. He played five sonatas by Scarlatti, Beethoven's "Tempest" Sonata, the Passacaille in B Minor by Couperin,

Liszt's *Au Bord d'une Source,* the Waltz in A-flat Major (op. 42) and Impromptu in F-sharp (op. 36) by Chopin, and Mendelssohn's Andante and Rondo Capriccioso. Reviews were positive. They also laid stress on the growing evidence of unusual mannerisms: twitching, humming while playing, lowering his head almost to the keyboard. Already a dedicated hypochondriac and mild germ paranoiac, Gould had been avoiding crowds and bundling himself up in the famed later manner since at least the age of six. Now, at age fifteen, the outward signs of genius were all in place. It is a word that would be applied, more and more frequently in the years to come, to the young man from the Beach.

But what, after all, is genius? Writers as diverse as Diderot, Artaud, and Pound would maintain versions of Aristotle's divine madness position—sometimes, indeed, tending to the far less plausible view that, just as all geniuses are madmen, all madmen are geniuses. Neither conclusion is borne out by the evidence, unless we are prepared to agree that any exceptional performance is by definition divine.

By this token, though, divine madmen seem to proliferate too far and too fast, revealing a familiar anti-divine double endgame. The trouble with genius is that there is always either too much or too little of it. In a logical extension of the elitist's rap on democracy—in the land where everybody's somebody, nobody's anybody—nowadays we have both too many geniuses and too few. So every successful investment banker is now a genius of finance, every talented cook a genius of fusion, every slippery running back a genius of rushing, every logo artist a genius of design.

On the other hand, the once solid geniuses of literature and philosophy, the canonical Great Names of the Great Books, are everywhere contextualized and historicized and otherwise cut down to size. They're not so special. Who do they think they are? *Genius* is exposed as a typical piece of Enlightenment self-congratulation, the regard of limited interests, maybe class-based ones, all dressed up as universal significance. In popular sociological texts of our own day, the exceptional is made ordinary, success analyzed in order to demystify it and make us all feel better. Now *genius* is just another word for someone who practises the ten thousand hours needed to excel at any given thing. No word, in these tautological accounts, on what qualities of gift or inspiration are needed to stay the course of those hours . . .

Satisfying though this may be to our self-regard, down here in the mediocre ranks, it seems ultimately unsatisfactory. The choice between an inexpressible gift from the gods and mere workmanlike persistence is typical of the age, a now-you-see-it, now-you-don't reduction. But what can we say in the face of it? How to avoid mysticism, on the one hand, and on the other what the critic Harold Bloom calls "historicizing and contextualizing the imagination of genius," the pernicious influence of "all those who would reduce authors to social energies, readers to gleaners of phonemes"?[32]

Bloom's special interest is literary genius—a category whose existence some people would be inclined to doubt.[33] We can nevertheless indicate some of the features that considered thinkers have ascribed to genius. *Fecundity,* first, since that is the root of the word: genius produces; it germinates. Also *vision:* an ability to see possibilities denied to the ordinary practitioner of an art, still more the ordinary fan or person in the street. Hence, too, *originality*—what philosopher Hans Jonas called "the intoxication of unprecedentedness." This quality makes genius an unstable property, since, if too little originality makes for mediocre work, too much originality risks incomprehensible work. Indeed, many consider genius to be that volatile reaction on the margin between sense and nonsense—a version of the madness theme again.

Finally, in literary form anyway, *irony* is commonly named as a distillate of genius, if not a strictly necessary condition for it. The genius appreciates the mortal finality of life, its inherent limit, even while making the most of life's ever-renewed powers of transcendence. These factors, or some of them, combine in the person of the genius, who creates work that, to quote Bloom, rises "above the age" and "buries its undertakers." Or, in poet Edmund Spenser's words: "Genius survives; all else is claimed by death."

So much may seem uncontroversial, if a little po-faced and tautological: does genius survive because it is good or is it good because it survives? And compare novelist and critic William Gass on the dubious blessing of meeting the test of time: "So works which pass the Test of Time are never again ignored, misunderstood, or neglected? No. Works which fail find oblivion. Those which pass stay around to be ignored, misunderstood, exploited, and neglected." The test of time is just a diachronic, transgenerational popularity contest, no more reliable than any other such.[34]

Any test-of-time account of genius also remains vague on the essential question of *what it is*. Further investigation reveals that the majority of genius claims are what a philosopher would call contrastive: genius is most often defined against something else, typically the concept of (mere) talent. Philosopher Arthur Schopenhauer, in his essay on genius, provides a standard contrastive account. "Talent is like a marksman who hits a target that the rest cannot reach; genius, one who hits a target they cannot even sight." In other words, "talent is able to achieve that which surpasses others' ability to perform, though not their ability to apprehend; it therefore immediately finds its appreciators." Genius, by contrast, may arouse a less positive reaction and may well be experienced even by its possessor as an ambiguous gift.

Once made, this conceptual lever has proven too powerful to resist. "Talent is that which is in a man's power," James Russell Lowell wrote. "Genius is that in whose power a man is." Oscar Wilde offered a variety of *aperçus* on the subject, including his much-repeated exculpatory claim that "Talent borrows, genius steals," and the self-regarding one that "Genius learns from nature, its own nature; talent learns from art."[35]

Wilde also made the following famous self-assessment concerning genius. "I put all my genius into my life; I put only my talent into my works." Some interpret this as an aesthete's call to arms, like Nietzsche's injunction to live one's life like a work of art. But Wilde is distinguished as a self-proclaimed genius—nothing in the canonical accounts of genius rules out such reflexive congratulation; some even demand it. In part because of that, he was well aware of the burdens of rising above simple talent. "The public is wonderfully tolerant," he noted. "It forgives everything except genius." Wilde defined genius as "an infinite capacity for giving pains," a neat inversion of the slavish "taking pains" of the merely talented, however perfectionist, combined with a puckish reminder of the way true genius can irk the status quo. He may have had in mind the formulation offered two centuries earlier by a fellow Anglo-Irish writer of gifts. "When a true genius appears in this world," Jonathan Swift wrote, "you may know him by this sign, that the dunces are all in confederacy against him."

This leaguing of mediocre interest against the genius was the central worry of John Stuart Mill, himself an oddball prodigy of such ability that his own mental powers threw him into breakdown during adolescence. "Precisely because the tyranny of opinion is such as to make eccentricity a reproach, it is desirable, in order to break through that tyranny, that people should be eccentric," Mill argued. "Eccentricity has always abounded when and where strength of character has abounded; and the amount of eccentricity in a society has generally been proportional to the amount of genius, mental vigor, and moral courage it contained. That so few dare to be eccentric marks the chief danger of the time."

But now a confusion has crept into the argument. First, we may not be prepared to accept the contrastive account of genius over talent. The categorical distinction proves loose on examination: where is the threshold between them, and who is positioned to judge it? Second, even if we did agree to such an account, the notion that genius and eccentricity are aligned, even correlated or coextensive, as Mill suggests, is overwrought. Not to mention the more controversial question of whether strength of character, mental vigour, and moral courage are implicated in eccentricity.

One does not have to count as a lackey of mediocrity to wonder whether eccentricity such as Gould exhibited is valuable in and of itself; sometimes it is pretension or fashion, sometimes no more than distinctive oddness—possibly charming, possibly not. Eccentricity may be a broad value in Mill's "experiments in living" conception of human freedom, the bare value of diversity, but any further claims will need more argument. Leaving aside the background questions of how eccentricity can be commanded ("people should be") and whether there can even be eccentricity without the concentric majority to support it—conceptually, first of all, but perhaps ultimately socially and financially— we must still wonder about a genius/eccentricity nexus, even as we find a genius/talent distinction slipping through our fingers.

More convincing, at least in their lack of conviction, are those views on genius that demystify it without reducing it to persistence. "Coffee is good for talent," Emerson said in his version of the contrasting pair, "but genius wants prayer." Gould, as we know, consumed a cocktail of prescription painkillers and anti-anxiety drugs in late life: coffee or prayer? Pablo Picasso, a man who knew a great deal about fecundity, was sharper: "Genius is personality with a penny's worth of talent. Error which chances to rise above the commonplace." And, reversing the usual polarity, poet Paul Valéry offers a crisp symbiotic account. "Talent without genius isn't much," he said, "but genius without talent is nothing whatsoever." This last point presumably goes some distance to explain the ranks of undiscovered artistic geniuses, most of them male and in their post-collegiate twenties, who throng the downtown bars and coffee houses of every major European and North American city.

Was Glenn Gould a genius? If we are prepared to be precise about the label, the answer is surely yes. Note that in Kant's *Critique of Judgment,* genius is not contrasted with talent—a mug's game, after all—but is instead defined as a special form of creative talent. "Genius is the talent (or natural gift) which gives the rule to art," Kant says, by which he means that genius is the quality of setting new standards in the aesthetic field, of being able to rewrite the rule book. The genius must be rare, because rules are not rules if they are broken every five minutes. The special quality of the genius is that he or she plots both the new trajectory *and* shows why the previous one was insufficient. In this sense, the genius performs a version of Thomas Kuhn's *paradigm shift*, whereby the new rules not only solve problems or explain anomalies the previous rules could not, but also show why they could not. (The problem may be mere repetition, the boredom of institutional stultification; the anomaly may be the existence of the genius himself.) Gould's blistering 1955 *Variations*, with its blithe omissions and apparent love of speed over emotion, broke all the rules about Bach; and in so doing, it rewrote those rules.

To talk about rules may be misleading in any case. "Genius is a talent for producing that for which no definite rule can be given," Kant goes on; "it is not mere aptitude for what can be learned by a rule." And so "genius is the exemplary originality of the natural gifts of a subject in the *free* employment of his cognitive faculties," namely, understanding and imagination. The notion of free play is key; it underwrites the mystery of the genius, who breaks the rules and so enters into a realm where there are none—along the way setting the new ones. For, in addition to originality, genius also exhibits exemplarity: it shows the way forward, in part by being sufficiently intelligible to existing standards as to avoid "original nonsense." Genius "cannot describe or indicate scientifically how it brings about its products, but it gives the rule just as nature does." Thus does Kant meld some elements of mystery—the genius cannot explain how he does what he does, or where the gift came from—with a modern appreciation that the genius is constrained by human limits.[36] Properly understood, *gift* is the right word: the gods of talent deliver gifts, to be received but never returned; we mortals only exchange presents.

Gould's genius was interpretive, but it is no less creative and groundbreaking for that, especially in the aesthetic realm of music, which can live only in performance. His influence is made inescapable; no performer after him can avoid the example he sets, an example derived from his original interventions and the arguments surrounding them. Now, everyone must perform *through* him; he can be emulated or rejected, but he cannot be ignored. It is true that sometimes Gould, like the ill-advised athlete conducting a post-game interview, attempted to explain what he was up to. He was more articulate than most people, let alone most athletes; neverthelesss, there is a constant danger that his theorizing will undermine the joy given by his performances. Indeed, the tension between these is a central facet of Gould's life, a tension that was never adequately resolved.

CHAPTER SEVEN

Quodlibet

The thirtieth variation in the *Goldberg* sequence is a quodlibet. The Latin word translates more or less as "anything goes" or, in more colloquial parlance, "whatever." In musical composition, the title quodlibet indicates a section that loosely incorporates snippets of melody, often drawn from folk songs or popular tunes, into the larger, more serious work. Bach's quodlibet does this, using two well-known German folk songs of the period as source materials; but the opening bars of the variation also offer one of the few places where the bass melody line of the entire composition is clearly stated. Variation 30, the catch-all or "whatever" variation, thus appears as a cheerful, serio-comic culmination of the entire sequence of play, drawing the varied threads together as we move into the final section, the aria da capo. It is a deliberately unstable penultimatum, at once forthright and ironic.

The notion of quodlibet also appears in the scholastic enumeration of divine transcendental properties. *Quodlibet ens est unum, verum, bonum seu perfectum,* medieval scholars argued. Which is to say: Whatever entity is one, true, good, or perfect counts as transcendental. The "whatever" here picks out something more mysterious than meets the eye. "Whatever" is not just a grammatical placeholder—whatever being it does not matter. It is also an ontological claim— there is a being *such that.* What is that being? The whatever being. Quodlibet is both pure singularity (the specific being) and absolute generality (all of these considered as possibilities). Quodlibet marks the abyss between example and class, act and potential, particular and universal. Individual beings can only be utterly singular because they are examples of a class that is, by definition, general. How is this possible?

Aristotle divides all potentiality into two classes: the power to be and the power to not-be. Of these, the latter does not seem to be a power at all, but instead an impotence. But the power to not-be is the greater, since it harbours within itself the other power and governs it, holding itself back in absolute potentiality. Thus the being that both is and is not itself is quodlibet being. As we can see, the whatever being contains already, in itself, the act of will (libet)—or rather, the potentiality of will, will suspended.[37]

The philosopher Giorgio Agamben phrased the issue thus: "Even though every pianist necessarily has the potential to play and the potential to not-play," he says, "Glenn Gould is, however, the only one who can *not* not-play." What can this mean? That Gould does not merely hover between playing and not-playing, as anyone might, but actively makes his not-playing a kind of performance—"he plays, so to speak, with his potential to not-play." Only Gould can do this because only he is so masterly that such second-order play becomes a possibility, albeit a paradoxical one. "While his ability simply negates and abandons his potential to not-play," Agamben concludes, "his mastery conserves and exercises in the act not his potential to play . . . but rather his potential to not-play."[38]

Gould gave his last public performance on April 10, 1964, in Los Angeles. He played four fugues from *The Art of the Fugue* and Partita no. 4 in D Major by Bach; Beethoven's Opus 109; and Hindemith's Third Sonata. He did not announce this as a final appearance, nor was it part of a planned farewell tour. Several other concerts were already on his schedule; he cancelled them all.

Though he had been performing publicly since the age of five, it was less than a decade since his American performance debut. He was just thirty-one years old.

The American debut concerts are legend, worth recalling in their immediacy and impact. On January 2, 1955, Gould played in Washington, D.C.; nine days later, he played in

New York. Gould was acutely conscious of the importance of these concerts and fussed over the repertoire, seeking a combination of pieces that would allow his technical prowess full display as well as distinguish his musical intelligence from the run of moody or bombastic Romantic set pieces thought suitable for an unknown's debut. Somewhat radically, he chose instead the "Earl of Salisbury" Pavan and Galliard by Gibbons, one of his favourite pieces and a winning confection of intricate structure and feeling. Also the Fitzwilliam Fantasia by Sweelinck, five Three-Part Inventions and the Partita no. 5 by J.S. Bach, Webern's *Variations* op. 27, Beethoven's Sonata no. 30, op. 109, and the Piano Sonata op. 1 by Berg. A very clever program, in other words, with some familiar pieces and some rare ones, all deployed with a mixture of high-percentile technique and a keen sense of musicality.

The Washington performance attracted only a small crowd, but the reviews were glowing. Critic Paul Hume: "January 2 is early for predictions, but it is unlikely that the year 1955 will bring us a finer piano recital. We shall be lucky if it brings others of equal beauty and significance."[39] Gould repeated the performance at New York's Town Hall, again to a small audience, but one with influential members. David Oppenheim, director of artists and repertoire for Columbia Records' Masterworks division, guided by musician Alexander Schneider, attended and was suitably impressed. He contacted Gould's agent, Walter Homburger, and offered an exclusive three-year contract—the first time he had signed an artist after just one hearing.

Of the resulting recordings, more later. For now, Gould continued to perform in public, indeed quickly stepping up his touring schedule to accommodate growing demand: it would spike after the first *Variations* was released later that year and would never decline. All the while, an increasingly familiar pattern began to emerge.

March 15, 1956: Gould made his American concerto debut and first performance since the 1955 recitals. He played Beethoven's Concerto no. 4 in Detroit with the Detroit Symphony Orchestra conducted by Paul Paray. Six curtain calls. But the reviews highlighted his odd onstage behaviour, his hunching and humming.

March 18, 1956: Gould played the concerto again in Windsor, Ontario. But this time he almost cancelled, his nerves frayed. He delivered only a mediocre performance. He played again three days later, with the Toronto Symphony Orchestra conducted by Sir Ernest MacMillan. He didn't perform for three weeks afterwards. Feeling "acutely distressed," he sought the advice of a neurologist at the Toronto General Hospital. He received prescriptions for Largactil and

Serpasil, drugs typically prescribed for mental and emotional disorders, including schizophrenia, but also sometimes used to treat insomnia and anxiety. Gould added these to the cocktail of drugs he was already taking habitually while touring to calm his nerves before and after performances.

January 26, 1957: Gould debuted with the New York Philharmonic conducted by Leonard Bernstein. His performance of Beethoven's Concerto no. 2 was a riotous success. Bernstein: "He is the greatest thing that has happened to music in years." Gould played thirty concerts in the subsequent season. The next year, fifty. Sellouts, runs at the box office, attendance records became common.

Summer 1957: The first overseas tour. Gould began in the Soviet Union, the first Canadian and first North American pianist to appear in post-Stalinist Russia. Gould's complex of fears were compounded and highlighted: of eating, of vomiting in public, of flying, of being overwhelmed by crowds.

On May 7 he gave his first performance in the Great Hall of the Moscow Conservatory, a solo recital of fugues from *The Art of the Fugue* and Partita no. 6 in E Minor by Bach, Beethoven's Sonata no. 30, op. 109, and the Berg Sonata. Barely a third full at first, the hall was crowded to bursting by the end of the performance, bolstered by intermission communication to friends. Gould was applauded for twenty minutes and played a long encore: a Fantasia by Sweelinck and ten of the *Goldberg Variations*. The audience was still clapping as the house lights came up, and Gould was later mobbed by admirers outside the concert hall.

May 8, 1957: Performance at the Tchaikovsky Hall with the Moscow Philharmonic. Beethoven's Concerto no. 4 and Bach's Concerto in D Minor. Sold out.

May 11, 1957: Tchaikovsky Hall sold out again, 1,500 people seated in the auditorium, plus another 900 allowed to stand or take chairs added onstage. The complete *Goldberg Variations* as well as two Intermezzi by Brahms and Hindemith's Third Sonata. Applause for thirty minutes.

May 12, 1957: Gould gave a seminar-recital on contemporary music at the Moscow Conservatory. Lectured on twelve-tone music and played Berg's Sonata, Webern's *Variations,* two movements from Krenek's Third Sonata. Some conservative professors walked out in protest, but the audience cheered. Encore: parts of the *Goldberg Variations* and *The Art of the Fugue*. Deafening applause.

May 16 and 17, 1957: Performances in Leningrad. Extra seats added onstage at Maly Hall for the first time ever. Police called to control the crowd outside the hall trying to obtain tickets. Gould played for more than three hours, including the entire Berg Sonata as an encore, and finally had to excuse himself in order to leave the stage.

May 18, 1957: The Bolshoi Hall, capacity 1,300, sold out. Eleven hundred seats added. Playing with the Leningrad Philharmonic, Gould offered Bach's Concerto in D Minor and Beethoven's B-flat Concerto. Encores and more encores. Gould took his last bow wearing coat and gloves. He later repeated the seminar-recital he performed in Moscow. Exposing students to twelve-tone music created, he said, "a sensation equivalent to being the first musician to land on Mars or Venus and to be in a position of revealing a vast unexplored territory to some greatly puzzled but willing auditors."[40]

Gould was now firmly in the grip of a tightening double-bind of performance. The more successful his concerts, the more pressure to repeat and even extend them. Nor were the concerts allowed to remain merely concerts. The wild displays of adulation grew, ratcheting up a nervous reaction on the part of the performer, second-order anxiety about his own reactions compounding first-order anxiety about specific fears. Parties, meals, travel, public displays of sociability—all these were the unseen external costs of performance.

May 24 to 26, 1957: Gould travelled to Berlin and played with the Berlin Philharmonic conducted by Herbert von Karajan. Performing Beethoven's Concerto no. 3 in C Minor during a rehearsal, he received an ovation from the orchestra. The concerts were runaway successes. H.H. Stuckenschmidt, a leading European critic, wrote: "His technical ability borders on the fabulous; such a combination of fluency in both hands, of dynamic versatility, and of range in coloring represents a degree of mastery which in my experience has not been seen since the time of Busoni."[41] Gould, by no means above flattery, memorized some lines of the review and later would often quote them to friends and colleagues—even as Stuckenschmidt likely stood as one of the inspirations for Gould's parodic music-critic character, Dr. Herbert von Hochmeister.

June 7, 1957: On his way by train to Vienna, the final stop on this tour, Gould encountered on the platform the conductor Leopold Stokowski, one of his heroes. He was thrilled to hear that Stokowski, a music-world celebrity who had married Gloria Vanderbilt, had an affair with Greta Garbo, and shaken hands on-screen with Mickey Mouse in Walt Disney's 1940 film *Fantasia*, had been following the young Canadian's meteoric rise. The two icons shook hands too, though off-screen. Later, at the Vienna Festival, Gould played fifteen Sinfonias by Bach, Beethoven's Sonata no. 30, op. 109, and Webern's *Variations*. The acclaim was universal, and Gould made a now-familiar final bow wearing his flat cap, overcoat, muffler, and gloves. From this point on, the cold-weather uniform was invariable and much reproduced—the outfit became Gould's favourite image of himself. The image's message extended beyond mere material fact, issues of low body temperature, or fear of infection. The message was this: no matter what the ambient temperature, it was always winter wherever Glenn Gould stood.

When Gould returned to Toronto on June 11, 1957, the Russian tour was already regarded as a triumph. He immediately went to New York to begin recordings of Bach's *The Well-Tempered Clavier,* even as he maintained a punishing concert schedule: twenty-two performances through the fall and winter. By the time he was about to embark on his second European tour, in 1958, he was so exhausted that his playing had noticeably declined, and on occasion, he surprised audiences by substituting pieces at the last minute, saying he had not practised the scheduled work enough.

Now began the steady declension of Gould as performer. Increasingly he cancelled scheduled performances, usually claiming ill health. He complained of sinus and respiratory ailments, colds caught from hotel air conditioning and worsening into tracheitis or even bronchitis. More and more time was spent alone in hotel rooms. Perhaps with good reason. The Toronto pianist Anton Kuerti, dining with Gould in order to cheer him up, ordered calf brains for dinner, and when they were brought to the table, Gould fled in distress.

Now the playing was suffering badly. On September 21, 1958, playing the Bach D-minor Concerto with Karajan and the Berlin Philharmonic, Gould anticipated his cue by almost a full second, throwing off the rest of the players. In October of that year, he cancelled all performances and confined himself to his room in the Hotel Vier Jahreszeiten in Hamburg, complaining of focal nephritis, a liver disease. He would later speak of the ensuing "semiquarantined" month as among the happiest times of his life. "Knowing nobody in Hamburg turned out to be the greatest blessing in the world. I guess this was my Hans Castorp period; it really was marvelous."[42]

A striking image. Thomas Mann's *The Magic Mountain* is the most musical of great novels, a sustained meditation on time, disease, and death, all executed by artful deployment of leitmotif. It is also a self-revealing exercise in phenomenology, a reflection on the fact of consciousness. "The book itself is the substance of that which it relates," Mann said of his work. "Its aim is always and consistently to be that of which it speaks." What is that? It is consciousness experienced as temporality—as both time and timelessness. The leitmotif, as Maurice Natanson has written, in both music and prose "is at once a gatherer, a displayer of what has been gathered, and an initiator of what is to come, given a particular complex of movements." Looking forward and back over theme and variation, working its way on us in time, "it portends and it retains" even as it "*presents* itself in immediacy." Retention, portent, and presentation: this is what Natanson calls the "triple play" of the experienced moment, the now.[43]

Castorp himself is a divided figure, a multiplying theme, by turns quixotic, arrogant, naive, sensitive, and shy. Perceived divisibly by the various characters to whom he is drawn, he is forever seeking himself in his symptoms. Perhaps, like Castorp, Gould should have stayed in his chosen sanatorium for an indefinite seven years, smoking cigars and listening to the gramophone, tossed between Settembrini and Naphta, falling for the girl with the Kirghiz eyes, forgetting his age, losing grip on his brilliant theories of time, letting his timepiece fall into disrepair. For when Gould ventured out on November 15 for a concert in Florence, he was booed for the first time in his professional life after playing a Schoenberg Suite. He considered cancelling a raft of performances, including a scheduled three-week tour of Israel—eleven concerts in eighteen days—but Homburger convinced him not to.

Gould returned to Europe just once more, in the summer of 1959. By now critical reception was focusing on his onstage manner, the late-hour substitutions, and the many cancellations. After his return to Toronto in August 1959, he would never leave North America again. Later that year he also decided, having recently passed his twenty-seventh birthday, to move out of his parents' house in the Beach, that semi-isolated bourgeois suburb of Toronto with its signature boardwalk on Lake Ontario, its open water and closed minds. At first Gould moved into a suite at the Windsor Arms Hotel, the downtown bastion of stylish tea-taking and apartment-dwelling. Designed in neo-Gothic style by Kirk Hyslop, it had opened in 1927 at the corner of St. Thomas and Sultan streets, alongside the University of Toronto's Victoria College, and had quickly become Toronto's favourite chapel of conspicuous conformity. (The hotel's sleek Three Small Rooms restaurant would not open until 1966.)

Gould then considered leasing a large country house, known as Donchery, some fifteen miles outside of Toronto, with two dozen rooms, a swimming pool, and a tennis court, but backed out at the last moment. Instead, early in 1960, he moved into the six-room penthouse of the Park Lane Apartments, a deco-style midrise on St. Clair Avenue West in Toronto. He would live here for the rest of his life, the solitude of the Hamburg hotel room now a daily possibility. He continued to book and play concerts but fewer with every year and with more cancellations. In the 1961–62 season he played eighteen shows, in 1962–63 just nine. In 1962 his fear of flying overcame him: he would never board an airplane again.

Agamben suggested that although in one sense Gould stopped performing, he did not and could not stop *playing*. Now the play was with his potential to play, exercised every day in the act of not-playing. The act of not-playing was distinct from simply failing to play, or happening not to play, or merely doing something else rather than playing. Gould's decision was not really a decision at all; it was instead an exercise of power, over himself and over music, which had to be renewed forever. He enacted not-playing for the remainder of his days, a continually reaffirmed mastery of whatever being. He was quodlibet man, pure potentiality. Playing music hid the silence that made music possible, the nothingness before, after, and between.

Gould played the silence instead. In this view, his not-playing, his playing of silence, may be understood as the greatest work of art he ever created, a life's work.

CHAPTER EIGHT

Competition

So Agamben read Gould's silence not as a kind of resistance but of activity beyond hearing. In this view, Gould was comparable to Melville's Bartleby the Scrivener and his gnomic utterance: "I would prefer not to." Bartleby, too, may be read initially as resisting, or refusing, the logic of transaction and performance demanded by office life under conditions of capitalism. But his preference is really a kind of stasis, reducing motion and speech by stages to nothingness. Bartleby dies, in a vagrant's prison. He is not Kafka's hunger artist, not quite comprehending his own refusals and withdrawals, seeking an approval and acclaim that has deserted him; Bartleby knows, to the end, where he is—and how he has got there.

With this final knowledge, Bartleby's inaction-as-action becomes an achievement of purity, a violent gesture free of determinant content. His "gesture of subtraction at its purest" (in philosopher Slavoj Žižek's words), where "body and statement are one" (in critic and author Elizabeth

Hardwick's) challenges the very idea of making sense according to the terms of sense that are presumptively accepted.[44] Agamben remarked with approval the suspended potentiality of this repeated statement of a *preference not to*. Bartleby's "perfect act of writing," moving from mechanical perfection to stasis, is a "pure act" of ever potentially not-writing. In the Arab tradition, Agamben noted, Aristotle's notion of agent intellect—thought without determination—"has the form of an angel whose name is *Qalam,* Pen, and its place is an unfathomable potentiality. Bartleby, a scribe who does not simply cease writing but 'prefers not to', is the extreme image of this angel that writes nothing but its potentiality to not-write."[45]

There are many versions of Gould's not-playing just as there are many of Bartleby's not-writing. Gould's own accounts of his concert-giving and its necessary suspension offer a variety of possible narratives. Other storylines emerge to supplement the medical and the philosophical ones suggested in the previous take. For example, he began his interview with the broadcaster John McClure by offering two distinct but not distinguished reasons for his withdrawal. After proclaiming the prospect of a return to performance "not enticing," he interrupted McClure's next comment, a staged incredulity that began: "The life of a glamorous concert artist . . . ?" "Is hideous, is dead, is part of the past," Gould leapt in to say. "I think that that has no relevance to the contemporary musical scene."[46] But hideous, dead, and irrelevant are not all the same thing.

Nevertheless, the key third argument he offered in his own defence was the barbarity of competition and the spectacle of performance more generally. Both competitions and performances are populated by what he called "the apprehensive listener," a listener who attends upon errors—raggedness in the strings, a muffed transition, an entry off by a fraction of a second. "There's a very curious and almost sadistic lust for blood that overcomes the concert listener," Gould said, a "gladiatorial instinct" that pervades the hall.

At the same time, those present are not qualified to engage in such apprehensive judgment. "Most people who go to concerts are certainly not musicians and care little about music, I think," he said. They go for some combination of atavistic reassurance—an illicit nostalgia that has nothing to do with music, that is "delusional" in its attempted proximity to music—and a perverse desire to witness imperfection so that the imperfection of their own lives may be negatively ratified. Gould denied contempt for this audience even as his own judgments, the very words of his articulation, made it obvious. The average concert listener, he said, doesn't know what he wants from a performance, any more than Gould knew whether he was "driving a tight or a loose car as a mechanic might define it."[47]

One's initial sympathies are likely to lie with Gould. There is something of the unseemly spectacle about all performance, the audience there to judge and react as the minority talented population—at the limit, a population of one—struts and frets its hour. We attend seeking pleasure or edification. The performer attends in order to provide them. Ideally, this should not be a zero-sum game, a competition; it should be more like an ideal contract, where each party comes away happy because each has attained a desired return on investment. Performers do not merely get paid, or paid merely in money. They derive pleasure from the act of giving the performance, of displaying talent and skill. That performers crave applause as a junkie joneses for his drug is axiomatic in this frame, a thought that assuages any lingering guilt we might feel about subjecting individuals to ruthless assessment and sometimes mockery.

Our sense of inferiority in respect of the displayed talent is structurally enabled by the concert set-up, with the performer elevated on a stage before the audience. But that inferiority is alleviated, even countermanded, by a second-order superiority inherent in the same set-up: the audience sits in judgment upon the performer. This superiority works along two distinct but related vectors. We disdain performers for the narcissism we assume underwrites their desire for the limelight; then, at the specific dimension, we feel entitled to judge the details of the performance. Thus the competition: even if there is nobody else onstage, the performer is being compared to some absent rival, even if it is one who exists only as part of a notional standard. Or, perhaps worse, sometimes the invisible competitor is the performer himself, invoked from prior performances—or even from no performances at all but instead from an imagined ideal, a reputational spectre.

No flesh-and-blood performer could hope to win such a contest. Is it any wonder that we speak of performers *dying* when they deliver a disastrous performance? Is it any wonder, contempt and anger returning back with interest, that a comedian will talk about *killing the room*? To be sure, a less common usage in the genteel world of classical music! But the impulse and the competition are the same. You come here and pay to watch me do this, whatever it is, because *you cannot do it*. And then you will cast judgment upon what you cannot do because that is what you *can* do, that right is part of what you have purchased. Thus does an agreeable contract conceal the zero-sum game beneath its surface.

Gould had more concrete complaints about the music world's insistence on performance competitions, especially with the glamour solo instruments such as violin or piano. He was the uneasy beneficiary of those competitions, arising like all prodigies from the sea of contestants and gaining the attention necessary to secure the next rung in a rigid ladder of success: a more prominent teacher, a recital with orchestra, a tour, a recording contract. He exposed the dark currents beneath the bright surface of the system. How easily we accept the win-lose logic of the competition, where someone's being first is possible only at the cost of all others not being so. How neatly we smooth over the pernicious effects of a novelty-mad system of musical desire, with those briefly famous Japanese ten-year-old violin wizards and teenage Austrian keyboard geniuses shunted into lifetime obscurity before they exit puberty.

From the other side, though, we might be inclined to take a different view. Was the genius of Gould not something larger than Gould himself? Did he not perhaps have a positive duty to share it, or at least not to withdraw it arbitrarily and without explanation? In fact, on the last point, Gould was quite ready and even eager to offer explanation. The 1968 spoken-word disc with McClure, *Glenn Gould: Concert Dropout,* lists on the cover a "partial agenda" that includes the following headings: The Concert Is Dead; The Only Excuse for Recording Is to Do It Differently; A Live Audience Is a Great Liability; Electronic Music Is the Future. (Also Why I Sing Along and Petula Clark's Songs Are in the Post-Mendelssohn Tradition, about which more later.)

On this record and elsewhere, Gould jumbled his objections into a confused and confusing mash of what looked more and more like desperate, if dryly delivered, self-justification. Live audiences create distractions and an atmosphere of dread. Concerts are obsolete because recorded music is widely available. Recorded music must be, in one sense, a recorded performance; but to create the illusion of seamless performance, it will be necessary to create multiple takes, employ spot-dubbing within takes, and rearrange timelines. The only justification for recording is to *subvert* the idea of the captured performance. And so the future lies in a perfectly electronic world where recording is realized without error or tic. At the same time, Gould indulged the tic of audible singing along because . . . well, because he could and because that put these performances under the sign of Gould. The 1964 *Time* magazine review quoted on the back cover of the album captures the paradox: "There is grace and good humour to all his recordings that make them seem like captured improvisations—personal, inspired, free. Such creative excitement is something few pianists can achieve."

Not just captured performance, captured *improvisations*! By refraction, we glimpse the unstable outlines of the Gould ideal: a recording so perfectly engineered and so carefully crafted, perhaps over hours and days of playing and mixing, that it sounds as though the player is making up the music as he goes. Gould never improvised for the microphone, unlike jazz or experimental players such as Michael Snow or Keith Jarrett (another notable devotee of audible humming while at the keyboard).[48] But he did appear to believe that interpretation and its attendant servant, the splice and take two allowed by recording, were a kind of improvisation. In a filmed conversation with Bruno Monsaingeon in 1976—a text of the dialogue was published in *Piano Quarterly*—Monsaingeon charged Gould, who often ignored or minimized dynamic changes, or refused to heed noted tempo markings, with wanting to "add an improvisatory element to all eighteenth-century music."

Gould pleaded guilty, cheerfully admitting that he eliminated sforzandos in Mozart's music, or arpeggiated chords that are written conventionally. "I imagine you do because they intrude upon your prerogatives as an improviser?" Monsaingeon asked. "I would have to go much farther than that, Bruno," Gould said. "I think they represent an element of theatricality to which my puritan soul objects."[49]

Gould was fond of saying that recording music merely allowed the musician the same freedom enjoyed by any other artist: a painter can change or cover a section of canvas, a writer can erase and revise. The analogy was not precise: Gould the performer was not the composer, even if his interpretations were judged themselves works of art. (As indicated earlier, I would so judge them.) The composer may revise a given piece as much as he or she likes; the composer is the only person entitled to say when the piece is done. The player is supposed to play the piece, and in some sense we retain an ethical-aesthetic right to expect that he or she can play it all the way through. Thus the idea, possibly atavistic but certainly persistent, that recording artists should at least be able and willing to play live.[50] Audiences regard such playing as a sign of authenticity, of artistic honesty—even if they also realize that authenticity and honesty may be unstable or dangerous categories.

We can observe the underlying instability here in familiar slippages from other art forms. A director and troupe of actors might decide not only to set a Shakespeare play in some provocative milieu—Romeo and Juliet as scions of rival California gangs, say—but also to cut whole sections of the authenticated text in the interests of brevity. These liberties are tolerated for a variety of reasons: leanness in the performance, coherence in the narrative. We accept these decisions, if we do, as called for or justified by the situation itself; that is, they are normatively inscribed in the demands of performance. This is a different form of acceptance from the one where, watching a film, we suspend disbelief about the actual time taken to film the various shots or the order in which they were done.

Film was Gould's strongest analogical point—it is no wonder he returned to it again and again, including his last recorded defence of the withdrawal, a 1980 multi-voice "fantasy" piece included in a twenty-fifth-anniversary disc done with Columbia. A player recording a piece may indeed resemble a director working with actors and a script, asking for take after take, ordering the actual playing as convenient under the aegis of the assembled whole being the piece in its correct order. And no director, even one who aimed for a highly artificial appearance of *reality* or *immediacy,* would consent to reproduce his efforts in some live manner. Indeed, given the nature of the medium, it is hard to imagine what that manner would be.

Gould lay on the cusp of a change in attitude to music. His career spanned the period in which recordings were, for the first time, reaching impressive levels of both accuracy and accessibility. He was bold enough to suggest that recordings are not best viewed as substitutes for live concerts, but are instead a medium unto themselves. This is correct. Where he erred was in thinking that this transition is a binary function: that the new medium will render the old obsolete. As McLuhan could have told him—indeed maybe did, on one of the several occasions they met or appeared together—a new medium does not replace an older one, it encompasses it like a new ring on a tree. Recorded music does not obliterate live music any more than television obliterates radio, or radio obliterates newspapers. Having made this elementary error, Gould's basic premise for the subsequent arguments against concerts was revealed as faulty.

The real reasons he was a "concert dropout" are not philosophical, they are psychological. That is not to say they are obvious or easy to understand. It suited him to take this stand, to enter a refusal to an established system: thus the use of the then-fashionable notions of dropping out and going electronic, Gould as classical music's version of Timothy Leary. But it suited him because he found performing unpleasant, not because he found it objectionable. The latter is a construct that at once justifies and conceals the former. And this concealment, apprehended at another level of his psyche, pleased this master of disguise and personae rather too much. Gould did not so much perform his *silence* as he performed his *refusal,* a juicy and endlessly repeated exit from the stage.

Nor is that all. The underlying irony is that Gould's apparent retreat into recording is actually the biggest competitive advance of all, one hinged on the technology of recording itself. Recorded music is what economists call a *scalable* activity: an individual effort that pays off over and over without further exertion. Reproduced and distributed on vinyl, a single musical session can capture a vast audience that was once necessarily divided among many in-person players. Every purchased Glenn Gould recording thus diminishes the chance of another musician being heard at all. Like bestselling books and blockbuster films, hit recordings are part of an inherently unfair winner-take-all market; the difference is that here the rivals are not just other books or movies, but other musical experiences in all forms. Talk about smoking the competition!

CHAPTER NINE

Time

All music has a time signature, ranging from the standard 2/4 and 3/4 of everyday experience to the esoteric deployment of 7/4 and 9/8 in some Bartok, 10/4 in Radiohead songs, or breakneck 19/16 in performances by Carlos Santana and the Mahavishnu Orchestra or Frank Zappa's Mothers of Invention. No matter what the signature's complexity, all music assumes as a precondition that time is both available and, more to the purpose, divisible. There could be no arrangement of beats and notes without these preconditions, and hence there could be nothing we call music. But what, after all, is time? And where, exactly, does its divisibility lie?

The great Scottish philosopher David Hume, in characteristic dashing fashion, deemed the question misplaced or mischievous. When we seek to examine the subject of time, we see nothing, for there is nothing to see. Time is an abstraction from experience that experience itself cannot grasp and thus an instance of the well-known tendency for ideas to run amok when undisciplined by skeptical philosophy. All knowledge save the logical and mathematical must derive from the impressions of our senses, and critical examination shows that we have no sense impression of something called *time*. Not least of the many important implications of this view is that what we call the self is no more than a fiction of memory, constructed from what we recall of past events; and that there can be no possible prediction of future events based on the apparent stability of past ones.

These conclusions may seem counterintuitive, but there is very little that reason is able to say in response to them—except to note an underlying problem in the assumption of the very idea of an experience. Hume posits a *succession of awareness* that is fabricated into a sense of self and temporality. But what is the condition of possibility for that succession of awareness? Must it not be precisely an *awareness of succession*? In other words, how can an experience even be an experience if there is not some grid of continuity and order that makes experience possible? The solution, Kant argued (answering Hume's "scandal for philosophy"), must be that time—and space—are pre-existing forms of sensibility that make experience itself possible. We do not experience these forms; they are the necessary presuppositions of any experience whatsoever. We cannot know them in the sense of empirical knowledge; but we can, indeed must, assume them to hold in order for there to be any such thing as empirical knowledge.[51] Glenn Gould, in common with any musician of gifts, brought this complex assumption closer to explicit articulation in the very act of playing. In fact, because some large part of Gould's play was play with time—fooling with tempo, obviously, but also with articulation, itself another name for the rich execution of tricky time-gambits—he revealed himself, again and again, as a master of sensibility. I said earlier that Gould *played the silence,* not the notes, including the big silence of the concert withdrawal. Is it perhaps even more apt to say that, after all, he *played time itself?*

But what then of the *exact divisibility* of time, that which appears to make such play possible in the first place? Without measure and division, music is not possible. In one view, such measure and division just is music, for sound so ordered makes for the structures and relations we perceive in composition and performance. An automobile's horn sounds a note—most often in the key of F or G, we're told—as does a seagull's cry; neither is music, though their tones can be found in music. (Leave aside the custom car horn that plays the first four notes of Beethoven's Fifth Symphony or the first bar of "Dixie.") When arranged properly, that is, on an ascending scale and within a time signature, these sounds create (the possibility of) music. The standard musical arrangement, graphically represented by the written score, is a negotiation with time as well as with sound: the staves have horizontal as well as vertical extension.

The conventions of the score did not emerge clearly until the sixteenth century, but were quickly adopted throughout Europe and were firmly entrenched by the middle of the seventeenth. Music itself, it goes without saying, is far older. In this sense, musical notation and its sense of temporal divisibility is analogous to the emergence of the reliable mechanical clock sometime in the twelfth century. Precise timekeeping devices, however useful, lacked the unit-based logic of the mechanical clock, which alone was capable of accurate equal measurement. The experience of time, and the practice of timekeeping, predate the unit of time: all civilizations have lived by the sun and moon, by the passing of the seasons.

Divisibility in timekeeping should therefore be understood as an emergent property of our lived experience of time, not a necessary condition for that experience, as it may retrospectively appear. In other words, we pause and consider our feeling of time having passed and then reckon that feeling into the units of some reliable metric. We find this useful and even necessary. But this division, like measurement in general, is performed via abstraction—another *post facto* illusion, however necessary. And naturally, once achieved, such abstractions offer immensely powerful instruments in the service of our varied human purposes. But they remain just that, instruments, and they rely on the unspoken presuppositions of their practices. Measurement and division are possible because of what philosopher Michel Foucault provocatively called the "contingent *a priori*"—not Kant's synthetic *a priori,* that is, but the non-necessary but assumed conditions of practical possibility. We can divide time not because of some unit-based essence of time, but because we assume the overlay of structure—simultaneously a form of violence and freedom, like all grids—on our suspension in the temporal.

There is an abyss between every note; a void looms in every interval. Measured time, musical time, is a wispy suspension across those voids. And then consider Count Basie: "It's the notes you don't hear that matter." Or Gould himself: "It [great music] is an ultimate argument of individuality—an argument that man can create his own synthesis of time without being bound by the conformities that time imposes."[52]

One is forced to wonder whether Gould, in the throes of his evident passion, actually enjoyed playing music. Not in concert, I mean, but at all. The question is not idle. In Bruno Monsaingeon's studio film of Gould recording the 1981 *Goldberg Variations,* one of the most impressive displays of genius in one medium caught by the deftness of another medium, we see a man lost in the music, lost in time, the supple fingering—he is forty-nine years old!—a sort of fine-grained climb across temporality. Transported, yes. But happy, exalted? Or, perhaps like the addict, a kind of willing prisoner of his own desires? Caught and freed at one and the same moment, at once controlling and driven, not taming time but pleading with it . . .

CHAPTER TEN

Architecture

You may have heard this claim: *Writing about music is like dancing about architecture.* In fact, you have heard it more than once, for this sentiment has been attributed to at least the following: David Byrne, Steve Martin, Elvis Costello, Miles Davis, Frank Zappa, Lester Bangs, Gertrude Stein, Laurie Anderson, Thelonious Monk, Brian Eno, Louis Althusser, Woody Allen, and Clara Schumann. Some dinner party that would make!

The sentiment itself is nonsense, though possibly forgivable nonsense. Few musicians like critics. Gould himself excoriated critics even while visibly craving the right sort of intellectual appreciation—one motive behind his creation of parody characters who would opine about his work. The nonsense extends along two fronts: first, that one should not want to write about music because writing is a medium distinct from music. In this view, the only appropriate reaction to music is more music, an absurd position if taken literally. Second, that the pointlessness of music writing is proved by analogy to the presumptive silly activity of dancing about architecture. But what, we may want to ask, is so silly about dancing about architecture?

Architecture has been defined as *frozen music,* a fanciful description but one that captures an essential insight. Architecture and music are alike in being extensions of structure across time; they are means of inscribing time in space. Kant's forms of sensibility are really no help here. Consciousness is the mysterious ability to spatialize time, to move a "self" through a metaphoric space. These metaphors are what make us human: metaphor is connection, it is the world-covering linkage of mind. The philosopher Henri Lefebvre, speaking in 1967, made the crucial point about the linkage between mind and world that is achieved through built forms: "Space is nothing but the inscription of time in the world," he said, "spaces are the realizations, inscriptions in the simultaneity of the external world of a series of times, the rhythms of the city, the rhythms of the urban population." Space, when experienced and shared in the form of public places, streets and buildings, is revealed as actually a form of *time.* "I suggest to you the idea," Lefebvre went on, "that the city will only be rethought and reconstructed on its current ruins when we have properly understood that the city is the deployment of time."[53]

The spatiality of built forms can sometimes obscure or overpower their enacted temporality, their gathering of time into shape. Most basically, we must exist with them moment to moment, day to day, even as we perceive at the complex, permeable margins how the building argues with its surround, its site and urban context. But a built form does more than this; it orders time-cradled consciousness into direction, movement, and use—what architects called *program*. A building is not like a painting, which seems to offer itself up *in toto* all at once, set off from the rest of the world by its obvious frame—though even this appearance is misleading, given how we must linger on the painting in order really to appreciate it, or how a given painting may work to subvert and overflow its frame. At the same time, music's apparent temporality, its being experienced in successive moments, can work to obscure *even as it delivers* our sense of the plan of the piece, the way it is built.

This last feature of music is what is meant by the architecture of a work, and the usage is not at all idle. *Arché*—the Greek root for arch—means "first principle," the beginning of the world. Architecture, the fashioning (*tekton*) of basic forms, is thus the most primordial of the arts, prior even to philosophy, at least in etymology. Without a first principle, there is no beginning; without an ordered beginning, there is no organization going forward. The same sense of necessary order is expressed in other places where architecture makes a metaphorical appearance: computer architecture, systems architecture, bureaucratic architecture (an ironic usage, perhaps).

Music itself, unlike built forms, is invisible in its architecture. That is one reason why an interpretive artist like Gould is no mere docent to a sort of tour of the musical building but instead a co-creator, almost an architectural partner. Music relies on the positive quality of sound, the audible punching of notes through vibrating air, for its realization. In this sense, we do not hear music. What we hear are sounds, notes in scattered progression, such that an underlying structure is somehow made evident—though not to the senses, rather to the intellect.

As a result, the musical experience is a complex entwining of sensible and intelligible, of (crudely) body and mind, as perceived sounds are organized by the hearer to replicate—or should we say embody?—the invisible structure that gives the piece its line. As Gould noted in the essay that accompanied the 1964 release of his "So You Want to Write a Fugue?" in an issue of *HiFi/Stereo Review,* "the persistence of fugue is evidence of the degree to which, acoustically and psychologically, certain devices peculiar to its structures—devices of subject and response, of statement and answer—are embedded within the consciousness of modern man."[54]

It would be a mistake to think, on the basis of these insights, that music is therefore entirely intellectual, or that simple or primitive sound-structures are insufficiently complex to deserve the label "music." Even patterned basic rhythms and song structures have contrastive elements to which embodied human consciousness responds; otherwise there would be no way to explain the enduring appeal of simple drumming, the three-chord progression, or the undemanding verse-chorus-bridge plan of much popular music.

Gould was especially drawn to musical architecture, as many highly intelligent musicians are. The mathematical beauty of baroque style, especially fugue, involves a refined intellectual pleasure. Or he sometimes was pulled by what was hinted at but not realized in the music. Gould said of Gibbons, for example, whose keyboard composition he labelled "half-hearted virtuoso," that "one is never quite able to counter the impression of a music of supreme beauty that somehow lacks its ideal means of reproduction."[55] Or he hinted at the existence of an idealized Bach lying behind its merely factual clavichord composition, waiting for the piano to draw it out. Gould spoke at many points as if he believed the ultimate reality of music to reside in its idea, the structure conveyed by the line. Hence one of the defences of his notorious humming: hearing the music in his head, he then transferred it to the airborne sensorium via the keys. But this expression was only a physical reflection of something mental, and the humming was likewise. At other moments, he was firm that music's reality is tactile and sonic, not ideal, that it does not exist apart from the playing. But what, exactly, do the tactilia of music reveal?

Praise of musical architecture can work to confuse a basic point about the reality of music. Unlike a built form, which realizes a plan in a solid and unarguable manner, the relation of a piece of music to its score, and of its score to its idea, is under constant review. That dynamic is entailed by the nature of performance, and the inextricability of music from performance. When we speak of the architecture of a piece, then, we are speaking both metaphorically and transcendentally. The metaphor is powerful, but the transcendentalism is misleading. Unplayed music is not really music, and however much we might admire the intellectual beauty of Bach's counterpoint structure, we cannot allow the reduction of music into mere thought.

The philosopher and mathematician Gottfried Leibniz's definition: "Music is a hidden architectural activity of a mind that does not know it is counting."

Arthur Schopenhauer's counter-definition: "Music is a hidden metaphysical activity of a mind that does not know it is philosophizing."[56]

Music may be mathematical, but it is not mathematics. It may be metaphysical, but it is not metaphysics. Play is not everything that music is; but without play there is nothing to hear. The thought of music is stillborn; the line of its composition goes unlimned.

CHAPTER ELEVEN

Play

I have argued: *Gould played the silence*. I have also argued: *Gould played the structure*. I have even argued: *Gould played time itself*. But what, in all this, do I or anyone mean by "play"?

"A happier age than ours once made bold to call our species by the name of *Homo Sapiens*," the social theorist Johan Huizinga wrote in 1938. "In the course of time we have come to realize that we are not so reasonable after all as the Eighteenth Century, with its worship of reason and its naive optimism, thought us." Other labels suggest themselves as a result: *Homo Faber*, man the maker; *Homo Economicus*, man the trader. Huizinga suggested *Homo Ludens*, man the player.

Play is found in every human culture, and in each one it is understood as that element that cannot be assimilated to any end other than itself. "The very existence of play continually confirms the supra-logical nature of the human situation," Huizinga claimed. "We play and know that we play, so we must be more than merely rational beings, for play is irrational."

Irrational, but not without reason, for play satisfies epistemic and physical needs that cannot be met in any other fashion. Play is voluntary, disinterested, endlessly renewable, and clearly set off from the other interests, categorical or utilitarian, that otherwise delineate human life. "Play lies outside the antithesis of wisdom and folly, and equally outside those of truth and falsehood, good and evil. Although it is a non-material activity it has no moral function. The valuations of vice and virtue do not apply here."[57]

Play is distinct from games, though it may well, and often does, form a central part of them. Games are structured forms of play and as such can succumb to the other valuations, especially virtue—the notion neatly captured in the bright line of difference between sportsmanship (virtuous) and gamesmanship (suspect).[58] Games themselves can be divided between *finite* games, those with a definite desired outcome, and usually some kind of time limit (including non-temporal limits like outs and innings); and *infinite* games, where play continues for as long as the engaged parties choose. Most sports, all competitive and professional sports, are finite games. Most children's games, some card games, and some forms of conversation are infinite games.[59]

Music occupies a special place in the world of play. As Huizinga notes, the verb *play*, denoting the manipulation of musical instruments, is found in both the Arabic language family and in the German-Slavonic family, a relatively rare East-West convergence that suggests the notion's deep roots in human culture. Music and play are alike in being impractical, transcendent, intangible, and ritualistic. In the ancient Greek world, the Muses governed far more than just the instrumental expression of harmony and rhythm; they were the inspiration for all forms of creative activity, including dancing and poetry, and the combination of order invoked by Apollo, Lord of the Muses, and Dionysus, guiding spirit of inspiration, made for the perfection of musical creation. For Plato, this meant the special vision—unruly and dangerous but also holy—which attended the divinely inspired; music might then have an ethical function, outer harmony encouraging the inner sort, but it was a volatile property. For Aristotle, musical perfection meant the privileged form of idleness that music marked: when playing or listening to music, no other activity is possible or indeed desired. Aristotle's notion of such contemplative idleness as the point of life, with work relegated to the realm of mere necessity, is scarcely retained in the spectacle of the weekend concert, the commodity of debased consumer leisure.[60]

Neither view survives the advent of modernity, but traces of both remain, and more than just etymologically. Even when no longer allied to the specific aims of a church or sect, non-vocal music remains the most ethereal of art forms, the one most immune from the didactic or representational traps that await artists working in other media. Its structural elements are more pliable than the twenty-six letters of the alphabet, weaving tone, rhythm, dynamics, timbre, and tempo—together with volume—into an apparently infinite range of possibilities. It is hard to imagine a more infinite game than the one we play at the keyboard, where every beginning and ending marks an episode but not an end, still less a victory or defeat.

Except, of course, that the score stands before us, an already scripted pathway through those possibilities. An interpretation may play with the precise margins and texture of the pathway, but it cannot deviate from it without, in some sense, ceasing to play the piece. This is why some musicians consider that only improvised performances really count as playing music; the rest is recitation. There is courage in this, a striking-off into uncharted—indeed, never to be charted, unless there is a recording—musical territory. The improviser makes it up as he or she goes along, and the basic temporality of music, the structure of anticipation and resolution, is even more firmly than usual placed in the negotiation of the moment, rather than residing—or perhaps hiding?—in the architecture of the score.

Calling other players fearful, the score their crutch, is going too far. But is there not something secure and comforting—something that enwombs the player—in the certainty of even a very difficult score? The piece cradles the player, who, in the playing, is safe from anything outside the score because there *is* nothing outside the score. The way is marked; one need only follow—if one can. And because playing the music exercises in the player, during these moments, the many hours of practice, the highly refined muscle memory of one mind's physical cognition, this play is actually a distillate of repetition. Gould strikes this one key this one time—attack and release—because he has struck that same key, in that same sequence, a thousand times before. This is the ultimate rest for the ultimate control freak, a safe haven of extreme difficulty traversed with calm mastery. Serious play.

CHAPTER TWELVE

Illness

It is not possible, now, to confirm the suspicion that Gould had Asperger syndrome, a form of autism that leaves cognitive and linguistic function relatively intact but manifests in anti-social behaviour and, often, distinctive physical tics.

The syndrome itself, first included in the American Psychiatric Association's diagnostic manual in 1994, is far from stable as a medical category: symptoms cover a wide range and often indicate other conditions. More seriously, the claim that Gould had the condition is now beyond the possibility of verification and, hence, is without a truth value. It is neither true nor false, and will remain that way forever. Nevertheless, Glenn Gould as Prize Asperger Exhibit remains a popular theory in efforts to explain—sometimes, indeed, to explain away—his combination of genius and peculiarity. Like many people with Asperger syndrome, but also like most first-rate musicians, Gould excelled at repetitive execution and feats of rote memory. He had limited interests and an intense, even compulsive focus on those few that drove him. He indulged in social withdrawal both privately and publicly. Certainly he had an eccentric personality. If his lifetime of devotion to his much-renovated Steinway piano, CD 318, is included, he may also have exhibited "idiosyncratic attachment to inanimate objects," as the diagnostic literature phrases it.[61]

All this proves nothing. Even supposing Gould did have Asperger syndrome, what difference can it make? It does not explain the appeal of his playing any more than a bio-mechanical, or indeed a sociobiological, account would. The only conceivable value in thinking that Gould was an *aspie* (as those with the condition call themselves) is so that he may join the list of gifted persons likewise thought to inhabit the category—a roster that includes, according to one cheerful source, philosophers Jeremy Bentham and Ludwig Wittgenstein, filmmakers Steven Spielberg and Tim Burton, mathematician Alan Turing, inventor Nikola Tesla, golfer Moe Norman, Philadelphia Phillies pitcher Steve Carlton, new-wave musician Gary Numan, and Pittsburgh native Andy Warhol.[62] Now here is a diverting sort of game to play with the idea of eccentric genius! Another, even more expansive list cites Jane Austen, Emily Dickinson, Mozart, Beethoven, Isaac Newton, Henry Ford, Kafka, Mahler, Nietzsche, Kandinsky, Alfred Hitchcock, Bobby Fischer, Bill Gates, Woody Allen, Bob Dylan, Al Gore, Keanu Reeves, and, in a double-play Steve Carlton would have appreciated, both *Peanuts* prime mover Charles Schulz and Muppets mastermind Jim Henson.[63]

Well, sure—why not? At this point, Asperger syndrome begins to resemble the proverbial mean-spirited society column, where the only thing worse than being mentioned is not being mentioned. What self-respecting creative person could resist having at least one or two symptoms to get them onto that list? Moreover, even if we assume that these lists enjoy some theoretical clinical validity—a large caveat, since they don't and can't enjoy any such thing—the invocation of Asperger syndrome as an explanatory frame is at this point discredited. No diagnostic category wide enough to capture that many diverse creative individuals, not to mention the many thousands of actually diagnosed but unfamous individuals, is narrow enough to tell us anything interesting about any one of them. For that, we have to look at them in the usual way, which is under the sign of their own achievements. There, and nowhere else, is the game of play played correctly.

Since the early 1950s Gould had been taking prescription drugs of various kinds, mainly for anxiety and associated bodily symptoms. By the end of his life he was also ingesting a varied cocktail of pills for blood pressure, anxiety, sleep disorder, and general unease. In addition to drugs such as Valium, obtained by prescription from various doctors, sometimes unbeknownst to each other, Gould took all manner of over-the-counter painkillers, sleep aids, vitamins, and dietary supplements. His self-medicating cycles were idiosyncratic and unpredictable, involving drugs taken to offset the effects of other drugs, the addition of new drugs to counter symptoms that emerged from the last drug, and so on. In the recording studio, right from the start, the colour-coded bottles and pills were as much a standard feature of Gould's apparatus of genius as the muffler and gloves, the curious chair, the arrowroot biscuits, and the bottles of mineral water.

This was no mere tic, however. Gould's hypochondria and general anxiety created a spiral of addiction in which symptom became indistinguishable from cure, where all illness was iatrogenic, the medication made into the disease. (Compare Roman poet Martial's ancient wisdom on the issue: "Before you came, a fever I had not. But then you saw me, thanks a lot.") Certain features of Gould's constitution were evident early, and this pharmacopoeia endgame can obscure the real suffering at its root. An odd incident in 1959 opens a chapter that ends only in the late 1970s and Gould's decline into death.

On December 8 of that year Gould was in New York to visit the technicians at the Steinway company. His beloved CD 318 was in need of an overhaul, one of several virtual rebuildings it would receive over its lifetime of association with Gould, who favoured the light action of its keyboard and the clarity of its sound. He would later joke that critics derided him for playing a piano that was tuned and balanced to sound like a harpsichord, but his reasoning here is very clear and in the service of his general philosophy of music. "I don't happen to like the piano as an instrument," Gould told an interviewer in 1964. "I prefer the harpsichord."[64] He had earlier said that CD 318 "is quite unlike almost any other in the world, an extremely solicitous piano with a tactile immediacy almost like a harpsichord's. It gives me a sensation of being so close to the strings and so much in control of everything, whereas modern pianos seem to have power steering—they drive you instead of the other way around."[65] On this occasion, speaking to several Steinway employees, Gould was greeted by William Hupfer, the chief technician, with a friendly slap on the back.

Accounts differ on how hard the slap was, whether it was indeed a slap, and so on. What is certain is that Hupfer made contact with Gould, who recoiled and began complaining of severe pain. Much speculation is directed at whether this renewed an early childhood injury to his back, when he fell in the family boat, or perhaps invoked it in some psychosomatic fashion. In any event, and despite a doctor's report that there was no evidence of injury, Gould began complaining of serious harm, claiming numbness in the fingers of his left hand as well as ache in the shoulder. It's possible the blow, or its imagined effect, aggravated a repetitive strain injury already troubling Gould. For his part, he claimed Hupfer had dislodged his shoulder blade. He began daily orthopedic and chiropractic treatments and cancelled numerous concert appearances even while, in other periods, he went on performing with apparent vigour.

In the spring of 1960 an orthopedic surgeon in Philadelphia, Irwin Stein, agreed to put Gould in an upper-body cast, his left arm elevated over his head. Gould assumed this bizarre hailing posture for a month, a period of discomfort that left him with an irrational dislike of the city of brotherly love, where he would cancel a concert the next year. Indeed, the Hupfer slap now provided Gould with an excuse to cancel or avoid any commitment he did not care for, from shaking hands with strangers to the entirety of his 1960 European tour.

It also gave him sufficient cause to bring suit against Steinway. Just two days short of a year after the slap, on

December 6, 1960, he filed suit against Hupfer and the company, demanding $300,000 in personal damages. The company responded by revoking his status as a Steinway artist and banning him from the Steinway hall. The following summer, in August 1961, the dispute was resolved out of court, with Gould finally agreeing to accept recovery of his legal and medical expenses: $9,372.35. He was restored to good standing as a member of the Steinway stable—but employees were now expressly forbidden to shake his hand. Backslaps are not specified but were, one imagines, suppressed *a fortiori*.

Eighteen years later, in June 1977, Gould began to experience a breakdown of control over his hands, numbness, and dysfunction similar to that resulting from—we cannot fairly say caused by—the Hupfer slap. This time, however, there was no Hupfer, and Gould was unable to externalize his unease, still less to sue anyone. Instead, and now characteristically, Gould internalized it. His diaries from this period show a long series of experiments, reported in pseudo-scientific language, attempting to diagnose the flaw in his physical mechanism. Gould dismantled his playing the way a slumping golf professional demolishes and then tries to rebuild his swing, even going so far as to alter his facial expressions as a way of shaking loose his wayward fingers.

The results were predictably unhappy. Despite the fact that some of Gould's most treasured recordings were still to come, notably of course the 1981 *Variations,* the diaries indicate that he never resolved the problem to his own satisfaction. The diary entries stop on July 12, 1978. Though he resumed recording in May 1979, and concentrated on radio production, conducting, and published defences of his various ideas, it may be thought that he was never again rationally satisfied with his playing. That he could play at all might be considered a victory. Other masters of repetitive movement often find themselves paralyzed by the press of analysis, such that the most habitual movement in the world becomes itself impossible—one thinks here of the golfer Ian Baker-Finch, whose career exploded when he could no longer execute his easy swing in competitive environments, or the New York Mets catcher Mackey Sasser, who one day found himself unable to toss the baseball back to the pitcher after a ball or strike.

Gould was well aware of this problem. In several interviews and publications throughout his career, he refers to it as "the centipede conundrum," from the childhood wisdom that a centipede knows perfectly well how to deploy its hundred feet—unless and until it is asked to explain how. "I don't want to think too much about my playing," he said when asked about, for example, his humming, "or else I'll get like that centipede who was asked which foot he moved first and became paralyzed, just thinking about it."[66] In repeated invocations of this wisdom, along with increasingly polished anecdotes about performing difficult pieces only with the aid of a nearby vacuum cleaner or radio or television, Gould attempted to defend an idea of music as essentially mental. That is, music's reality is abstract and it is recalled or reconstructed in the mind as the necessary condition of performance—which is now considered at best the smooth and unobtrusive vehicle of music's delivery. Indeed, we can note here how often Gould, the passionate driver, uses vehicular metaphors to discuss music: a good piano is like a car with rack-and-pinion steering; a good performance is like a tight rather than loose car in a competitive race. And in one of the cherished anecdotes—told at least three times in print and dubbed by author Geoffrey Payzant "The Chickering in the Desert"—Gould describes driving his Hertz rental car into the Israeli desert in order to put himself back in touch with a piano action he likes, and so to think his way back into performing comfortably on a slack-action piano he encountered in Tel Aviv during his 1958 tour of Israel.[67]

When performance becomes conscious of itself as performance, the lucid mediation between thought and

GLENN GOULD

sound is broken, and the tripping begins. Thus the necessary distractions offered by closed eyes, bodily swaying, humming, and even external noise—though with the last we surely approach the margin of unintelligibility, since, as Payzant notes, "Not even Gould's most faithful readers could be expected to agree that music sounds better when it cannot be heard."[68] Even those of us exercising much lesser gifts of physical coordination can appreciate the basic problem, and do so even if we are not persuaded by this version of Gould's musical idealism (which was in any case inconsistently maintained). Thought becomes the enemy of action when action depends on second nature. "Don't think too much out there," a coach will tell his baseball players, well knowing that a pause for reflection between pitch and swing, or between contact and shortstop, is the recipe for error.

The curious thing about this danger is how much thought is implicit in the very idea of second nature. Aristotle appreciated the full force of the problem, even as he argued for the rationality of ethical action: in most cases, the desirable action will come as a matter of *phronesis*, practical wisdom or know-how, not extended philosophical reflection. But this know-how—one of the main virtues of thought—is itself the distillate of painstaking thought and investment of time. You have to do the reflecting first, as well as imitating and practising what is good. Then, and only then, will you be ready to act rather than to think, to act in a sense without thought but really *beyond* thought. In successful performance we become vessels of the desirable, not articulators of it. Articulation would, at that moment, prevent success.

One can speculate endlessly about the causes of Gould's late-career breakdown; everything from the recent death of his perfectionist mother to the routine pressures of middle age has been cited. And it is surely the case that his hypochondria, combined with the cycles of self-medication, anxiety, and (importantly) the means to indulge these, created its own toxic energy. But I think the simplest explanation is both the best and the most frightening. Gould was caught in a control freak's nightmare. Even as he struggled to fix something he felt was broken, he was attacked by new waves of misgiving about whether the steps he was taking to solution were actually making the problem worse. Not only was his playing stalled by thought, in other words—he had become the centipede—but, far worse, the thought itself had become stalled, recursive and self-negating at every moment. This is the energy of consciousness bent back upon its bearer.

There was, and could have been, no resolution to Gould's malady because, by its own definition, resolution could only mean further thought; and thought was itself the malady. There is no cure for that, because, even were he able to frame this last thought, the one concerning thought's self-violence, no escape is thereby made available—except in the obliteration of all thought, of the very fact of consciousness. Until then, there could be only further imprisonment in the labyrinth of reflection.

CHAPTER THIRTEEN

Puritan

Music has been thought sacred. It has been thought edifying. It has also been viewed as a site of struggle, an agon both personal and social.

Despite music's allegedly divine provenance, its players have, for most of recorded history, met with indifference or even disdain from their audiences, their abilities even sometimes rated as a form of menial labour. Aristotle considered musicians vulgar and untrustworthy—the ancient sanction for the still-common view of the player as, well, a player. Until very late in the history of the West, music-makers could claim a status no higher than domestic servants. "In the 17th century a prince kept his musicians as he might keep his stable," Johan Huizinga notes. "Everybody knows that even Haydn still wore livery at the Esterhazys and received his orders daily from the Prince."[69] The silent reverence and programmed applause of the contemporary concert hall is of a very recent vintage, and may with time be regarded as one more blip in the history of music's production and appreciation. What once was a boisterous and some-times drunken scene of performance and revelry, the medieval banquet hall, developed into the less lively but still unrapt chamber-music evening at court and, from there, via the long inevitable arc of democratization, into the secular church of the modern symphony orchestra or staged piano recital, with its strict rituals and code of manners.

Beneath the polite surface of the audience, in whose number a cough or sneeze may be considered unacceptable, there runs a deep silent current of confrontation. Those who decry—rightly enough—the pressure-cooker music contests of our era, where besuited youngsters, perspiring over violins or pianos, are set against one another like so many performing animals, might care to remember that head-to-head competition has been a feature of music at least since Apollo stood against Marsyas to see whose lyre skills were superior. Centuries later, in 1709, Cardinal Ottoboni set Handel and Scarlatti against each other, wielding harpsichord and organ respectively. In 1717 Augustus the Strong, king of Saxony and Poland, arranged a contest between J.S. Bach and a non-entity named Marchand, who had the grace, or wisdom, not to show up. London society was abuzz in 1726 because of the struggle between rival Italian singers Faustina and Cuzzoni.

Nor is the competition restricted to individuals and their abilities. Musical taste is a social marker, a sign of position and sophistication. Tiffs between schools or composers dominate the eighteenth and nineteenth centuries, and Gould himself arrived on the mid-twentieth-century music scene amid a lively battle over twelve-tone composition, of which he was an early proponent despite the apparent bias in his recorded work for baroque and classical styles. His half-century lifespan ranged over the massive proliferation of new popular music styles, together with the arguments, put-downs, fashions, and disdain that are so much a part of anyone's engagement with popular music, the stuff of late-night disputation and rude magazine columns.[70] While Gould, like most classical musicians, was largely immune to the sort of argument that pits fans of one group against those of another, closely similar group—Freud's narcissism of minor differences crossed with Veblen's insatiable desire for social distinction—even he could not resist the impulse to praise Petula Clark in contrast to the Beatles.[71]

The gist of his typically puckish and verbose argument, delivered as a 1967 essay for *High Fidelity,* was that Clark's music, especially "Downtown" and "Who Am I?," was in the post-Mendelssohn tradition, effectively joining down-beat sentiments with upbeat melody, while the Beatles' quasi-orchestral experiments struck him as meretricious. "They went about sabotaging the seats of tonal power and piety with the same opportunism that, in *Room at the Top,* motivated Laurence Harvey in his seduction of Donald Wolfit's daughter," he wrote of the Liverpool quartet. "Their career has been one long send-up of the equation: sophistication = chromatic extension. The willful, dominant prolongations and false tonic releases to which they subject us . . . are merely symptomatic of a cavalier disinclination to observe the psychological properties of tonal background." If his tendencies were not already clear, Gould went on to note how "coffeehouse intellectuals" had taken up the Beatles in the 1960s just as they "talked themselves into Charlie Parker in the forties and Lennie Tristano in the fifties."[72]

It is against this kind of cultural-critical background that we must assess Gould's claim to be "the last puritan." In 1976 he published in *High Fidelity*—now something of a house organ for Gouldian *pronunciamenti*—an interview with himself. (Part of this interview is dramatized by Colm Feore in one of Girard's *Thirty Two Short Films About Glenn Gould.*)

This was not the first time Gould had indulged this particular conceit. He had done a shorter self-interview, in 1972, about Beethoven, in which he (or "he") analyzed "schizophrenic tendencies" in his playing of the great romantic composer's music, which he did not like, as against Gibbons's, which he emphatically did. The main point is that one may play a disliked composer well, but only apparently at some psychic cost.

The later self-interview was more wide-ranging and expansive, a summing-up of Gould's late-career thoughts about recording, performance, the future, and music. It was filled, perhaps to overflowing, with his particular brand of self-referential wit. The most striking feature of the performance, however, was a sudden veering into moral and political territory just past the two-thirds mark. After explaining that battleship grey was his favourite colour, the interviewed Gould was asked by the interviewing one whether he was in favour of censorship. "You do realize, of course, that you're beginning to talk like a character out of Orwell?" he said. To which the answering Gould responded, "Oh, the Orwellian world holds no particular terrors for me. . . . It's the post-Renaissance tradition [of individual freedom] that has brought the Western world to the brink of destruction. . . . It's only in cultures that, by accident or good management, by-passed the Renaissance which see art for the menace it really is."[73]

Art is a menace because it separates word from deed, encouraging a perception that there is no harm in words alone, together with a predilection for moral qualification that allows us to minimize our own inherent violence. Thus Gould's claim, made here as a repetition of an earlier assertion, that he, "rather than Mr. Santayana's hero," was *the last puritan*. It is a peculiar assertion in more than one way. Even his own contemporaries might have found the allusion a bit esoteric, if not precious; later readers would find it baffling. The American philosopher George Santayana, perhaps most famous for saying that "Those who cannot remember the past are condemned to repeat it," is known for his skill in writing essays but not for writing fiction. His autobiographical 1935 novel, *The Last Puritan,* is now almost forgotten, but it was a resounding success with readers at its time. Indeed, it ranked just behind Margaret Mitchell's *Gone with the Wind* in the bestseller lists of mid-1930s America. The main character, Oliver Alden, embodies an inner conflict that Santayana believed typical of twentieth-century America. Alden, replicating many of Santayana's own experiences, is torn between a sense of pure duty derived from the Puritan tradition and the desire-machinery of the new materialistic age. In effect, the story is a sustained critique of the tragic incoherence of that ideological bill of goods, the American

Dream. (It is worth noting in passing that Santayana, an able and prolific aphorist, had this to say about music: "Music is essentially useless, as life is: but both have an ideal extension which lends utility to its conditions." A sentiment with which I agree, even if Gould might not.)

As with most of his provocations, Gould made his assertion more than once. It became part of his personal mythology and his standard self-display. In addition to recurring mentions of puritanism in general, Gould's claim to being the last one was repeated in a film script for a 1979 CBC documentary about Toronto. When made, the film contained a now-celebrated scene of Gould singing Mahler to an elephant at the Toronto Zoo; it also received perhaps the most devastating one-liner review in television history: "Dracula lives as tour guide to Toronto."[74] Gould's youthful good looks, approaching beauty, were in full evidence on early Columbia LP covers; he had by the 1970s unfortunately declined into a ghoulish heaviness, balding and large-spectacled, possibly in part as a result of drug use.

Gould's original script for the film was almost 45,000 words—for reference, about 10,000 words longer than the present book—but was cut down for filming, and an abridged text was published in 1981. "But you have to understand that, as an anti-athletic, non-concertgoing teetotaller, I approve of all [civic moralistic] restrictions," Gould said in the film. "So I always felt that 'Toronto the Good' was a very nice nickname. On the other hand, a lot of my fellow citizens became very upset about it and tried to prove that we could be just as bad as any other place."[75] Like most Torontonians, Gould felt moved to defend his hometown only when those from elsewhere criticized it. A letter (September 18, 1964) from William Wright, then editor of *Holiday* magazine, to Montreal novelist Mordecai Richler made this clear: "I had dinner last night with Glenn Gould," Wright wrote, "who is full of curiosity about you. He thinks you are a meany and a bully. I assured him you were neither, but just felt Toronto was improvable."[76]

In the midst of this Torontocentric meditation, then, the large claim: "I, perhaps, rather than the hero of George Santayana's famous novel, am 'the last puritan.'" It is not at all obvious what this means, whether Gould was really suggesting kinship with Oliver Alden or merely using a phrase whose general resonance he liked. Whatever his actual knowledge of Santayana's novel, though, I think we can say that Gould sought here to identify with one important strand of the Reformation tradition. He wanted to see all aesthetic judgments as, in fact, moral ones, and regarded the notion of individual freedom, especially as a mere function of desire, with suspicion. Thus his reported pleasure in eliminating theatrical elements from Mozart's music. Yet Glenn Gould was, surely, in his cloud of hyper-conscious self-presentation, disappearing, and posturing, one of the most theatrical people who ever lived, the Garbo of St. Clair Avenue. Like most puritans, he was a dandy of his own convictions, fussy, precise, and censorious. The reverse relation also holds true: every dandy is a puritan of *his* own aesthetic convictions. From this vantage, Gould's increasingly elaborate image-projection—the habitual clothing, the spectral existence as a nocturnal monk of art, telephoning and recording in solitude—veered close to camp.[77]

At the same time, Gould was genuinely tortured by a sense of duty to something other than himself, acutely conscious of the duty of genius. These ethico-aesthetic commitments were now deployed as one more variation on his perpetual theme of why he no longer performed. The interview itself, he said, was just such a play of variation upon theme: though we seem to have left the ostensible subject (concert performance) for another one (freedom and censorship), in truth we have been circling back upon it, again and again, all the while.

So what, exactly, is the theme? "It's simply that, as I indicated, I've never understood the preoccupation with freedom as it's reckoned in the Western world. So far as

I can see, freedom of movement usually has to do only with mobility, and freedom of speech most frequently with socially sanctioned verbal aggression, and to be incarcerated would be the perfect test of one's inner mobility and of the strength which would enable one to opt creatively out of the human situation."[78] He would willingly submit to such imprisonment, provided certain conditions were met. The cell would have to be painted battleship grey. And he would have to maintain close control of the humidity and temperature settings, because of his tracheitis.

At this point, the interviewing Gould suggested that the real imprisonment—and hence the real hoped-for canonization—could only be enacted by a return to Salzburg Festspielhaus, where the tracheitis was first traumatically contracted. "There could be no more meaningful manner in which to scourge the flesh, in which to proclaim the ascendance of the spirit, and certainly no more meaningful metaphoric *mise en scène* against which to offset your own hermetic life-style, than to define your quest for martyrdom autobiographically, as I'm sure you will try to do, eventually." The interviewed Gould hotly denied he had any such desire, dodged the suggestion of a return to Salzburg, and brought the interview to a close with a reference to the signature line of Billy Pilgrim, from Kurt Vonnegut's *Slaughterhouse*

Five—Gould had recently done the score for George Roy Hill's 1972 film version, which he deplored for its "pessimism, combined with a hedonistic cop-out"—by saying, "I'm not ready yet."[79]

What are we to make of all this? The self-interview form destabilized the ideas even as they were delivered, and the conflicts contained in the notion of a last puritan—a difficult, perhaps tragic, mixture of self-congratulation and self-disapproval—were quartered, or splintered, by the forced interplay of the two voices. Gould accused himself of a desire for immortality even as he allowed himself free rein in articulating an anti-individualist philosophy at odds with his own aggressive choices. His desires were not at all straightforward, in other words, and not in any simple fashion such as experiencing a mere inner conflict about returning to the stage.

The almost hysterical glee with which the interviewing Gould offered this suggestion—the prison sentence guaranteed to achieve martyrdom—made this amply clear. The various dodges and feints of self-justification that Gould had tried at other recorded points, taking on the criticisms made against him—of narcissism, of aggrandizement—were now turned into Möbius strips of ironic dialogue, by turns accusing and justifying, serious and mocking. There was psychic conflict on display here, to be sure, but it was labyrinthine and, to use one of Gould's own favourite words, aleatory: it was a series of performative gambles, implicating the reader or listener in the presumed game. That is why the one thing we can confidently conclude from this curious document is that, in the mind of Glenn Gould, this is indeed a kind of intellectual fugue.

In the psychological lexicon, a fugue state is characterized by selective amnesia, loss of stability in personal identity, and the formation of new identity. Unexpected travel or wandering is typical—sudden disappearance. Gould never suffered amnesia, but his fugue-like intellectual wanderings were themselves evidence of a condition. If he was the last puritan, it was less because of any special disapproval of this or that feature of the modern world and more an unwillingness to take up one of the usual stable positions within that world. A fugue player is not in a fugue state, of course, but Glenn Gould was certainly forever disappearing.

CHAPTER FOURTEEN

North

In 1967 Gould broadcast on CBC Radio, as part of Canada's Centennial celebrations, a groundbreaking voice-based documentary called "The Idea of North." It was to become his most famous composition.

The idea behind "The Idea of North" was a mixture of form and content, also of dialogue and mood (much of the dialogue is inaudible because of deliberate cross-mixing). In form, this was the first example of Gould's contrapuntal radio. The voices of the documentary would not be arranged in the usual linear way, one following the other, intermixing to create an overall narrative or logical whole. Instead, they would rise and fall over each, creating layered effects where a given voice might not be distinguishable. Gould described the desired effect as something similar to the experience of sitting on a subway car or in a crowded diner, hearing snatches of conversation, creating a whole not from a logical plan but from the intervention of listening as a creative act, as a sort of retrieval.

In these terms, "The Idea of North" is at best a partial success, since the listener feels controlled and frustrated at the same time. There is no real chance of intervening as a listener, except in the sense of straining after a falling voice, losing its sense whether you like it or not. Nevertheless, the program is a remarkable piece of radio, brave for its time—complaints about its inaudibility, entered by casual listeners, indicate this much—and partly cogent in its background ideas. That is, it is always interesting, if not enlivening or enlightening, to test the bounds of linear construction.

Inversions of linear expectation are arguably more illuminating in visual media, however, where we have a chance to arrange and rearrange the parts as we go forward in the temporality of the experience. The screen defines the edges of what is presented, even if the presentation is in montage or split screen. Radio, like music itself, is a medium of more sustained and rigid involvement on the part of the audience: it is a fundamentally intimate medium, an interior experience. (McLuhan was correct about this difference between visual and aural media, even if his language of "cool" and "hot" is misleading and imprecise.) In the face of Gould's production some listeners are likely to feel helpless, if not vexed, by the constant rearrangement and fluctuating voice levels, even if they appreciate its roots in modernist experimentation.

Contrapuntal is not quite the right word, either; despite Gould's claims that the piece was constructed on the model of a fugue, it does not in fact offer the satisfaction of resolution to a tonic (whatever that would be in these terms) or even the meta-satisfaction of deliberately dashing the expectation of resolution to the tonic, as in Goldberg Variation 15, with its three prolonged rising right-hand notes . . .

In content, matters are more compelling. In a later recorded piece, a somewhat strained fantasy of Gould confronting his critics, one of Gould's own personae, Professor Karlheinz Klopweisser, would suggest that the real counterpoint is ideological, between the exercise of individual freedom and the "tremendously tyrannical force" of the *Zeitgeist*. In freely seeking isolation, choosing to be "in the world but not of the world," the various figures in Gould's documentaries enact a "double counterpoint resolved at the octave."[80] We can think of this, naturally, in terms of Gould's own withdrawal from the world even as he remained fully engaged with it via sound recording and the telephone, those emblematic media of communication in McLuhan's age of acoustic space.

We could also think of it, more generally, as an example of what the critic Edward Said labels "contrapuntal consciousness." This is the experience of anyone who dissents from a dominant world view, sometimes as a function of visible difference crossed with ideology (for example, skin colour interpreted as "race"). In both cases, however, it is not always easy to discern a resolution of the kind offered by clear contrapuntal musical structure; rather, we glimpse something that such structure, in music, only hints at, namely that the real lesson of all counterpoint is not that it resolves but that it only appears to—that the play of layered and contrasting voices must begin again, ever again, always renewed.

"The Idea of North" was the first of three pieces in Gould's *Solitude Trilogy,* a suite of heavily edited radio works that also includes "The Latecomers" and "The Quiet in the Land," about the inhabitants of a Newfoundland fishing village and a prairie Mennonite community, respectively. All three are documentary in a minimal fashion only. Gould was cheerful in his admission not only of elaborate editing but also of some manipulation in content, suggesting for example that the fourteen characters presented in "The Latecomers" were all related. The voices are, in fact, less real people than ideas or sentiments, aspects of thought— personae. They have been shaped, if not distorted, by the aims of the overall work, just as Gould the recording artist would treat the elements of a musical composition.

And so Professor Klopweisser's suggestion that Gould leaves the characters behind: "you create a dialectic in which their polarities are united," he tells Gould in the later radio piece; "you create a collective recognition of the argument that binds them together." This is placed in direct rejection of what another persona, Sir Nigel Twitt-Thornwaite, calls "integrity of the unique and unrepeatable moment captured forever" and which Gould mocks as, instead, "the embalmed concert moment" and "the permawaxed record-ing moment."[81] As so often, the work is not, or not only, about what it is about. "The Idea of North," indeed the whole trilogy, stands as another in a long series of Gould manifestos about the value of sustained artificiality over (alleged) captured authenticity. That this argument is deliv-ered with Gould himself using at least three, and sometimes five, different voices is precisely the kind of irony he found excessively amusing.

The voices that animate the first work are people who live in and know Canada's vast northern territory. They speak of their experiences with humour, political sharpness, and some-times weary familiarity about how the rest of the country ignores or neglects their home. One of them mocks the idea of "northmanship," whereby a given person tries to outdo another with feats of isolation or deprivation: if you have gone on a twenty-two-day sled-dog journey, I have completed one of thirty days, a game with no theoretical limit. And yet, as he noted, "It's not like there's some special virtue or merit that comes from being in the north."[82] Another plays with the idea of natural beauty, remarking how often and how inevitably it is filtered through prior perception of reproduced images. All of them, speaking on radio, are aware of the structural irony that isolation at once removes them from the overwhelming volume of mass media and makes them available and connected to it.

More than four decades later, not much has changed. Indeed, if anything, Canadians are more indifferent than ever to the realities of life in the largest area of the country. Global climate change and fossil fuel depletion have made the region more significant than ever, with shipping and resource opportunities that are not being ignored at all by other sovereign powers, especially the United States, whose purchase of Alaska may be about to pay off once more with a viable Northwest Passage. Meanwhile, the great majority of Canadians have not visited the region and don't intend to, huddling instead in the string of medium to large conurbations scattered across the country's southernmost edge. It cannot be any surprise that policy with respect to the north is a mixture of embarrassing misunderstanding and condescension. This simply mirrors the attitude of most Canadians, which, when it even rises above indifference, tends to see only an abstraction wrapped in clichés tucked into a boring enigma.[83]

These matters were not really Gould's concern, of course, especially the policy issues—he held no brief for Aboriginal land claims, environmental protection, or sovereignty. To that extent, he fell into the same romanticizing trap that afflicts many artists who try to speak for a region or people but instead end up creating an exotic image that cannot help but be partial or even demeaning. Gould was mostly fetched by the idea of north as a category of thought, a philosophical idea. The real north was not the subject of his thinking, even if the subjects of the documentary hail from there; the subject was, instead, the metaphorical north. The title, indeed, tells us as much.

And it turns out that north is, more or less, a synonym for solitude: consciousness is here a function of latitude. North was not for Gould, as it is for some of us, a negative frontier, a pushing-down of hostile weight, the large uncharted fact of human-killing cold that defeated Hudson and Frobisher and the rest and, along the way, negatively defined Canada as a nation. In this common view, our cities are fragile bulwarks against the weather, contingent timeouts from the constant effort of the climate to obliterate us. Instead, what exercised Gould's imagination, and ours as we try to follow the weave of voices in the documentary, is what it feels like to be isolated and often alone: to have no company other than your own thoughts. It is not a reference Gould would likely have known, I suppose, but here he echoed the adolescent dream of Superman's Arctic headquarters, the Fortress of Solitude, paradigmatic secret clubhouse for one, complete with library, laboratory, chess-playing robot, and exercise equipment. (The last, at least, not on Glenn Gould's wish list.)

The theme of solitude would continue with the second and third entries in the emergent trilogy. In a country as large as Canada, with so small a population, solitude, not company, would seem to be the natural condition. And yet, the vast bulk of the population not only does not live this way, it never even considers the places where people do. Thus the real subject of contrapuntal radio, a form that demonstrates incomplete or illusory dialectic resolution in ideas, is Canada itself. The country is unpacked by the documentary and revealed as a postmodern nation of widespread contrapuntal consciousness—postmodern because here there is no dominant *Zeitgeist* to escape, no hegemonic culture, only the proliferation and expansion of consciousness itself. This view of Canada, not unique to Gould, would remain influential during the last decades of the twentieth century and it is still a central piece in the never-ending puzzle called Canadian identity.

Is the preoccupation with isolation a psychic projection of Gould's own desire to elude the company of others, the flesh-pressing presence of people's bodies, their breath and heat crowding in upon him? Is it an excavation of a larger psychic cavern, the national unconscious, which keeps its own deep fear of loneliness at bay by constructing not just cities but the logic of survival that supports the frontier conception of the north? Is it, more existentially, a reminder of the essential solitude of every person, who must die alone because my death is something only I can enact—others can watch but no other can do it for me? Is it all of these, wrapped in contrapuntal layers not of voice and sound but of thought and its absence, the silences of solitude and of the final fact, the end of the piece, death? Yes.

But what of the implicit meaning of north, the need for hospitality? A harsh environment—any strange environment—throws us onto the thresholds of strangers, asking for food and shelter. In the ancient traditions of nomads and settlers, the demand for hospitality could not be refused: I had to admit the stranger to my home, had to offer him a share of my wealth and security. The stranger was my revered guest precisely *because* I did not know him. In Latin, *hostis* (enemy) and *hospitis* (guest) are rooted in the same otherness, the novelty of the unknown person—and thus the two hosts hosted in our own tongue, the one who welcomes his guests and the other that is the army, sometimes the heavenly one, which fends off the enemy. Hospitality, so often now removed to the hygienic realm of the service industry—the hospitality suites and hospitality mints of the hotel industry—retains in its etymology a hint of the real stakes.

The dwellers in Canadian towns and cities know this still, if only in crisis. When a stranger's vehicle is stranded in the snow. When a pet or child is lost in a storm. When we recall that the security of reliable shelter and ready supply of food is a collective achievement, though deployed under the sign of the isolated individual. The north bespeaks solitude only against the backdrop of shared risk. To be alone requires that we share, that we achieve together, the conditions of solitude's possibility. Did Gould appreciate that, making all those late-night telephone calls to distant friends, his shadowy interlocutors? Was that his form of welcome?

If so, was it enough?

Communication

In his *Piano Quarterly* review of Geoffrey Payzant's 1978 book about him, Gould faced down the mild psychoanalyzing in which Payzant had indulged here and there within the pages of his mostly philosophical study.

Citing psychologist Anthony Storr's now-classic study *The Dynamics of Creation,* Payzant had made this suggestive point: "Since most creative activity is solitary, choosing such an occupation means that the schizoid person can avoid the problems of direct relationships with others. If he writes, paints, or composes, he is, of course, communicating. But it is communication entirely on his own terms. . . . He cannot be betrayed into confidences which he might later regret. . . . He can choose (or so he often believes) how much of himself to reveal and how much to keep secret."[84]

Gould retorted: "This citation seems indicative of Payzant's own attitude in regard to his subject and adroitly summarizes Gould's abhorrence of city life, his distaste for public appearances, his predilections for telephonic communication, his belief that solitude nourishes creativity and that colleagual fraternity tends to dissipate it."[85]

Later in the review, he mentioned in wry tones Payzant's hint—it is no more—that Gould's fondness for psychoanalytic imagery might indicate a history of analysis. "Given that Payzant and Gould are both residents of Toronto," Gould noted, "and that this sort of speculation could presumably have been settled with a simple 'yes' or 'no', such inconclusive testimony—verging, indeed, on idle musing—can produce a rather comical effect." Except, one wants to interject, that there is no *simple* yes or no here. "But its obverse," Gould went on, "is that quality which lends to Payzant's book its greatest strength—the author's obvious determination to prepare his portrait without being interfered with, or influenced by, the conversational connivance and media manipulation at which Gould is allegedly a master."[86]

Alleged by whom, exactly? By Gould, in a review of a book about himself? By that book, or by some other, unnamed, book? By some generalized anonymous "they," Martin Heidegger's *das Man*? In the end, Gould praised Payzant with the full force of his habitual irony of uncertain direction. Any critic could, he said, simply accept "the conventional image of Gould as an eccentric and erratic pianist-pundit." Payzant had wisely chosen, instead, to "harmonize" Gould's "musical predilections, moral persuasions, and behavioral extravagances," in the process fashioning "a texture as structurally secure and chromatically complex as the baroque fugues which first awakened Glenn Gould to the wonder of the art of music."[87]

The review itself surely has fugal elements, even if the book in reality does not. Gould's play here is multilayered and self-conscious to a degree well beyond the easy use of that solecism of the media age, referring to oneself in the third person. That is merely part of the review's basic conceit. In addition, he is indulging media images of himself even as he—apparently—ridicules or distances himself from them. The concluding show of praise is itself a fiction of the review's performance, for at least two obvious reasons. First, there is no clear substantial difference between the so-called conventional view and the one he attributes to Payzant: both work to explain Gould's eccentricities in the context of his music, explaining one by reference to the other. Thus, Payzant's view is tarred with the same brush—or, perhaps, accepted as equally valid; it is not easy to say—as the usual ones. Second, even supposing a clear difference, the attribution of structural harmony to Payzant's view is heavily backhanded, carrying a strong whiff of mockery. Payzant, Gould suggests, has imposed on his life the same sort of "cheating" structural narrative resolution that Gould brings to a recording, or that a composer brings to a counterpoint composition.

What is being communicated here, then, beyond Gould's routine show of cleverness?

His competitive streak, for one thing. Gould slighted Payzant for mentioning family reminiscences of his childhood will to win at croquet on the cottage lawn in Ontario, his fondness for driving powerful cars aggressively, his penchant for playing the piano with tour-de-force prowess—this despite the repeated claims that competition was anathema to him, and to music. On croquet at least, the critic had a point. Anyone who has played croquet, especially at a summer cottage or in the garden of an Oxford college, knows that it is among the most vindictive of games. Among other things, it is fair play to choose to send your opponent's ball rocketing into the undergrowth in place of attempting to advance your own. "Payzant seems determined to uncover inconsistencies in Gould's attitude," Gould remarked mildly. But of course this is the ultimate competitiveness, that of ever having to have the last word, the higher forms of which tendency Gould displayed constantly in his late written work and conversations. Gould was a player in more than one sense: he was devoted to the disinterested possibilities of art's openness, sure, but he was also a ninja master of literary one-upmanship and sly evasion. Whenever confronted by a contradiction, he slid smoothly by it, ideally while delivering a sneaky counterpunch to his accuser in the form of feigned offence—the feigning as important as the offence, since he would not wish to be pinned down even to being offended.

Gould was still more skilful in his adoption and manipulation of views about himself, many of them of his own provenance. These were juggled like so many beachballs, biffed and swatted but never rejected or answered, their legitimacy forever deferred by the performance. Thus did Gould communicate an unease with himself, the truth, and himself in relation to it. In fact, there could hardly be a more elaborated example of Storr's schizoid type, revelling in the combination of isolation and communication as a means of controlling that which is revealed.

The most significant phrase in the Storr quotation is, however, the parenthetical one in the last sentence: "He can choose *(or so he often believes)* how much of himself to reveal and how much to keep secret." Gould's tone in this review, as in all his written work, especially the self-referential pieces, has an element not just of performance—he was not a natural writer, his tone always pedantic or defensive—but of self-delighted smugness. He sounds like one of those suavely accented James Bond villains who revel in explaining their plans for world domination before eliminating the pesky licence-to-kill agent in some overly elaborate fashion, possibly involving lasers and miniskirted henchlings. Like them, what is revealed in the explanation is not control but the *desire* for control, which in being revealed is also by the very same action thwarted. Real control means never having to worry about being either understood or misunderstood.

In fairness, Gould communicated a great deal more than this in the simple execution of his role as a performer of gifts. That much is clear to, and cherished by, even the most casual fan of his playing. The question is, What, precisely, is communicated by such playing?

Not meaning. Non-vocal music has no propositional content. We may speak of it as a language, with a grammar, but it remains a language that, even if in some sense intelligible, cannot be translated into any other. Though we may investigate music to learn about culture, or history, or ideas, music itself carries no message; though perhaps beautiful, it is mute.[88] That is why many philosophers, notably both Kant and Hegel in rare overlap, praise poetry more highly, since it joins the emotional suggestiveness of harmonics with the precise articulation of truth. Many people, especially those of romantic persuasion, will find such ordering invidious, since for them beauty is truth, truth beauty, and that is all you know on Earth, and all you need to know. Or, if they are of more Platonic persuasion, they might even think that beauty is a form of goodness. Thus non-linguistic beauty is considered just as valuable, if not more so, than the kind offered with words. Beauty is its own message, its own unanswerable argument.

The irony is that the beauty-goodness claim is advanced in written dialogue, even as the truth-beauty claim is made in a poem, in language; this is often lost on these romantics. In any case, we need not pause too long here to dismantle the many problems in so claiming a co-extension of the concepts *beauty* and *truth*. The English literary critic I.A. Richards used the last lines of Keats's famous ode to illustrate the prevalence of "pseudo-statements" in poetry and suggested that anyone who accepted this as an aesthetic philosophy was likely to "proceed into a complete stalemate of muddle-mindedness as a result of their linguistic naïveté." But Richards was too hasty: it is not a pseudo-statement; grammatically, it's a regular old statement. And as a statement it is either just false (lots of true things are ugly, and vice versa) or it is nonsensical, i.e., neither true nor false, lacking a truth value (as we say). And if it is the latter, then it is the statement of a pseudo-proposition, not a pseudo-statement.

Well, who cares about any of this? Significantly, Glenn Gould. Two things emerge clearly from his recording practice. First, that he believed strongly in the truth of an interpretation, as a revelation of the given work's essence of potential. And second, that he had a strong, almost compulsive urge to share these interpretations, together with their attendant intellectual scaffolding, with as many people as possible.

In this view, it is not at all difficult to make sense of at least one of the stated reasons for the 1964 concert withdrawal. Gould was now endeavouring to spread his musical ideas far and wide, with no theoretical limit beyond the scope of reproduction. Nor is it hard to accept one of the corollaries of that decision, namely, that it is wrong not to share "the future"—meaning by that *both* existent and imminent playing or recording technologies *and* future potential audiences—with great works of the past. The now mostly uncontroversial decision to play Bach on piano, for example, was from his perspective no different from a decision to record with splicing and multiple takes or to consider the possibilities of synthesizers for recording classical music. (Though he was dismissive of gimmicky versions thereof, such as the briefly celebrated novelties of P.D.Q. Bach and Switched-On Bach.)

Gould's sense of truth in interpretation was therefore inescapable in his playing, even though he did not subscribe to the romantic notion of a beauty-truth fusion. From a certain point of view he was more interested in bringing out the essence of the work than he was in whether it was beautiful; this, I think, accounts both for his ability to play pieces he did not like and to judge works based on aesthetic criteria that are, in fact, moral ones—something he admitted, indeed claimed, on many occasions. This is truth in a very loose sense, given that non-vocal musical work can have no truth value. But things without meaning can nevertheless matter, and the task of the player is to bring out the matter-not-mean potential of the work, paradoxically to give its muteness a compelling voice. We might call it rightness rather than truth. And we might say that music, like language, is a container for consciousness.

In our own day, perhaps, such ideas are as uncontroversial as those about the ethics of recording. We no more suspect abstraction and free play of concepts than we do the standard techniques of the recording studio. Yes, dedicated projects of playing "early music" on "original" instruments, tuned flat or rescued from obscurity (the sackbut enjoys a vogue on American college campuses), are very much with us. But these strike many people as eccentric if forgivable foibles, slightly more reputable versions of the Renaissance Fayre or Klingon Opera festivals held regularly in city parks. There is no fundamental or originary truth to be had about a piece of music, no definitive authentic rendering that once and for all communicates its message, and so the quest for one is misguided *prima facie*. Gould knew that, and so defended *his* interpretations as compelling rather than cognitive or authentic; as accurate and intense renderings of the original concept. He did this at some length in his written work, to be sure, but all that verbiage is beside the point: these rational addenda are really just after-the-fact rationalizations, at best footnotes or clues to the actual argument. The only argument that matters is the argument offered by the playing itself.

What kind of argument? The answer to that is, I think, very hard to put into words without making music the servant of some master other than itself, which will never do. Perhaps it is best to proceed negatively: this is not an argument with a conclusion, though there may be resolution in the performance; it is not an argument with a point, though we may find it inspiring to hear; it is certainly not a normative argument, though we may decide, hearing it, that we must change our lives.

So then what? In a sense, it may be understood as an argument with time itself. The essential paradox of music is that, as a medium, it holds time open. Most media of communication are premised on the nullification of either time, or space, or both. Formerly it took a month for a letter to reach Europe from America; now an email is there in mere seconds. Time shrinks in communication just as space shrinks with speed: the commonality between communication and technology is that both are driven, in almost every instance, by the imperatives of speed. Speed closes distances, we say, because it allows traversal of space in less time: velocity is no more than distance divided by time. Like all divisions, there is no theoretical limit to it. The asymptote of all speed projects is the state in which time and space are so fully collapsed that all points are the same point, and therefore no interval stands between them.

Music resists this: it draws time out, holds time's obliteration at bay, with its deployment of artful sound and silence. We say that music communicates grandeur, or sadness, or elation, or wit. Strictly speaking it can do none of that, since it is not a medium of communication. We are speaking metaphorically: music suggests these emotions or ideas, arouses in us a response we characterize in that fashion. I argue that it performs these suggestions, or allows their entertainment in audiences, precisely because it is not communicative, because there is no proposition or truth-value in play. Whatever else it does or may do—arouse emotion, tickle the intellect, satisfy the sense or the soul—music refuses the obliteration of time.

That, finally, is the only argument music can make. Gould, performing the argument, knew that it was enough.

CHAPTER SIXTEEN

Appearance

Gould argued that a musical recording was like a film; that he was akin to both the players and the director; that the final result was a kind of artful deception, a recorded aural transcript that could smoothly, over and over, create the experience—the illusion—that one was hearing the music as it was composed, in the moment. In a succession of moments. What kind of deception, what species of illusion, is this?

The mistrust of appearances is deeply felt in human experience, an evolutionary advantage surely at or near the heart of our success as a species. No wonder it has been thematized by philosophers East and West from antiquity to our own day. Our apprehension of the world is suspect because, again and again, we discover that things are not as they seem. We wake from real-seeming dreams. We pull bent sticks from water to find they are straight. We ride close enough to a tower to see that it is square, not round. We reach for a coin upon the floor and find that it is merely painted there.

The last technique, called *trompe l'oeil*, expresses the stakes with rare forthrightness: *the trick upon the eye.* We are fools for semblance, and our only hope lies in recognizing our folly as a first step to its remedy.

And what lies on the other side of this wall of mirages? The philosophers say: the thing in itself. True knowledge. Ultimate reality. Transcendental Forms. Essences. Foundations. Noumena, not phenomena. Originals, not copies. Objects, not images. Plato's well-known hostility to the distortions of *mimesis,* mere imitation or reflection, shadowy mirroring, is not lately given the sort of free rein the Greek philosopher favoured, when such suspicion is elevated into an elaborate system of epistemological hierarchy. But the basic orientation remains, possibly hard-wired into our problem-solving, adaptive consciousness. We want to punch through appearances to find something more reliable. We won't get fooled again. Except, of course, we will.

Gould's polemics about recorded music must be seen against this fundamental context of thought, as well as in the contemporary cultural surround. As the concert died its slow death, the once primary vehicle of music supplanted even if not destroyed by the long-playing record, the compact disc, and the digital computer file, the idea of the single-take performance lost its presumptive authority. Early experiments in recording, which simply captured a single performance so that it might be replicated anytime, at any distance, gave way to techniques of recording that created an illusion of single performance out of the raw material of multiple takes, over-dubs, splices, and even electronic tempo manipulation. The question is, Does it matter?

To answer, we must specify what kinds of false appearances are possible. The most common cases are ones of simple perceptual or cognitive error, such as the optical illusions and dreams just mentioned. These errors are dispelled by a change of frame. But what of *intended* deceptions in appearance? Here we can distinguish at least two common types, of which Payzant offers a vivid example: an automobile without an engine is, to all outward appearances, no different from one with an engine.[89] Because the motive force of the car is invisible under ordinary circumstances, those circumstances give us no means of judging the presence or absence of that force. We only discover the false car's lack of functionality when we attempt to operate it. No amount of looking will do the job. So the appearance is misleading but in a manner dependent upon the project of future use. By contrast, a copy of an Old Master painting passed off as original is deceptive in one step: it wears its deception all on the surface. Either we see through it at the level of looking, or we do not; there is no function test, no second step. The forged painting *pretends;* the engineless car *hides.*

A person, meanwhile, being capable of active deception, may *dissemble:* that is, he or she can pretend as well as, and perhaps precisely in order to, hide. I wear a false smile to cover my falsehood, say, or dress as a businessman as part of my campaign of sociopathic serial murder. At the same time, the complexity of consciousness means that we are capable of deceiving ourselves as well as others: the *delusions* of false consciousness, bad faith, or repressed desire.[90]

Which of these—pretending, hiding, dissembling, or deluding—describes Gould's idea of the fiction of a recorded musical performance? None, I think, though we might at moments be inclined to say one or more of them. Instead recorded music offers a clearly distinct kind of appearance, that of the achieved whole constructed of discrete parts *whose material origin is made irrelevant.* This form of appearing is not hiding, pretending, dissembling, or deluding. Music is just exactly what it appears to be, no more and no less, in two important respects.

The first concerns origin. We might think that recorded music is a sort of dissembling, since it feigns an appearance of sequential creation. Except that there is nothing concealed beneath the surface, since music is all on the surface. A closer analogy in interpersonal relations would be not dissembling but role-playing or self-presentation. Now, there may be considerable complexity in the deployment of a given social role or roles (good son, flirtatious partygoer, dependable professional), but there is no intention to deceive and no structure of concealment. There is, instead, what we recognize as play—in persons as well as in art. The materials of a painting, the pigment and oil or water or tempera, create an appearance of a face or a landscape, or just of forms; the earthly elements are fashioned in such a way as to play at looking like something, but we do not *distrust* them for that. The material elements of music, which are arranged sounds and silences, are all the more cleared of the charge. They simply are whatever music is; no suspension of disbelief, however minimal, is requested.

The second concerns originality. Unlike a forged painting, which is parasitic on the copied original, there can be no false pretense in music's presentation, since no claim of originality or authenticity is advanced. To think otherwise is, in effect, to imagine that all art is crudely mimetic, as if every representational painting forever longed to achieve the executed deception of *trompe l'oeil,* to be so indistinguishable from the thing itself as to fool the bird who tried to eat Zeuxis's painted grapes. Music and abstract painting, not being representational even in outline, should be especially immune from this odd charge, and even representational painting is ill-served by the thought. To judge paintings on their mere fidelity to nature or sitter is naive. As one of the characters in Gould's "The Latecomers" remarks, great art aims to articulate ideas—universal themes—by means of particular details that do more than merely represent, that maybe surpass representation altogether. "Well, let me put it this way," he said. "Perhaps *The Last Supper* is the greatest abstract piece of art ever produced."

A critic might object that there *is* a claim of originality and authenticity in recording, made by implication. That is, we listen to a recording with an unstated presupposition that the performer is executing the performance as we hear it, captured as if by accident on the microphones and transferred to vinyl or digital code. But such naïveté is hard to maintain with a straight face. Gould's film analogy is solid here: only a child imagines that the two hours of a film are captured in exactly two hours of filming (the actress Tatum O'Neal once confessed to this illusion). And even a child understands that there is willing suspension of disbelief involved in the execution of the simplest cut or pan, the skilful framing of action and sequence. Narrative art, unlike life, can skip time. Why should music not, in its execution of time, compress and rearrange time? Moreover, this attention to honesty is aesthetically misplaced from the start. Wilde: "In matters of great importance, the vital element is not sincerity, but style."

A more controversial version of the appearance/reality debate comes in Gould's claim that his studio manipulation actually offered a *better* version of a given piece than could be achieved in single performance. But this, too, survives scrutiny. The sound editor's art consists in drawing out the most compelling interpretation of the composition, aligning the elements seamlessly so that the whole unfolds not only without gaffe—even the most accomplished performer will make a mistake now and then—but without aesthetic defect. Editing serves the performer's vision; and, if we trust his thought and skill, this art in turn serves the composer's vision. The appearance is the reality, now in both superficial and deep senses: there is nothing beneath the audible surface, and therefore no gap to be suspicious of. The music is all we hear, but it is also all that we are meant to hear.

Which leaves just the nagging worry that the illusion will fail, that so far from being seamless, the construction of the appearance will intrude upon our awareness and so destroy the aesthetic moment. Gould's own experiments in this field are convincing. In 1975 he gathered a group of professionals and amateurs into a CBC studio and set them the task of detecting splices and other editorial interventions in various recordings. Among other results, in some cases false positives outnumbered true hits by three to one—possibly an artifact of the structured suspicion in the experiment, but nevertheless indicative. And guesses tended to sort by expertise: musicians tended to distrust colouristic effects, such as sforzandos, pedal changes, or instances of rubato; sound engineers were drawn to ambient-volume dips; while laypeople favoured paragraphic thinking, hearing splices in movement shifts or at the end of passages.

In short, even the trained human ear cannot reliably detect the presence of edits. "The tape does lie and nearly always gets away with it," Gould asserted; and in this quarter "a little learning is a dangerous thing, and a lot of it is positively dangerous."[91] Conclusion? We should abandon for good the habitual appearance/reality dichotomy.

Conversion may take only an instant. Looking back over a quarter-century of studio recording in 1975, Gould recalled the day in 1950 when he was presented with a soft-cut acetate of his radio network broadcast, of works by Mozart and Hindemith. At that moment, he said, "I realized that the collected wisdom of my peers and elders to the effect that technology represented a compromising, dehumanizing intrusion into art was nonsense." That was "when my love affair with the microphone began."[92]

There is no reality beyond what appears. You really can believe your ears. What else?

CHAPTER SEVENTEEN

Progress

Not the least of the many tensions or paradoxes in Gould's thought concerns the notion of progress.

On the one hand, he was deeply suspicious of, and even sometimes openly hostile to, the logic of supersession that is implied in typical narratives of progress, especially in art, where the new is presumptively judged the better. This was especially true of the avant-garde/traditionalism energies of his first years as a professional musician, when he saw his own fleeting enthusiasm for musical modernism subject to the dreary mechanics of fashion. Case in point: in 1951 the composer and conductor Pierre Boulez published an essay in *The Score* in which he declared "*Schoenberg est mort*," a once-revolutionary artist swallowed up by his own attempts to merge twelve-tone technique with romanticism. Gould recalled this polemic as "a singularly nasty little temper tantrum," but it was clear that he, in a very different way from Boulez, was also dismayed by the arc of Schoenberg's career. Reviewing a biography of Boulez a quarter-century later, in

1976, Gould noted with obvious relish that Boulez, in turn, had become "a victim of the zeitgeist," subject of a logic of displacement that saw him supplanted in the cultural moment by Karlheinz Stockhausen or John Cage.[93]

The curse of the *Zeitgeist* is not so much one's being driven to innovation, but rather having one's driven innovations made the subject of fashion. These notions can be hard to untangle, especially given all modern art's imperative to make it new; and so part of the curse is confronting that very difficulty. How much of a Schoenberg or a Boulez is a function of chasing fashion rather than being brutalized by it *post facto*? How much of what counts as radical innovation so counts because of its decision to oust the conservative status quo? Because the answers will always depend on our own sympathies and influences—our own sense of ourselves within a larger narrative—we, too, are victims of the curse. Gould suggests that the ultimate product of this curse, the familiar story of rising radical fallen to reactionary ruin, is "the archetypal product of the American Eastern Seaboard's megalopolitan mentality."[94] We might more simply call it, after Adorno, "the culture industry." That story, in fact, rather than innovation, is the real product of the industry, that which we happily consume.

So Gould sought, with some success, to evade this narrative logic, though a critic might say that he merely expressed its conservative counter-energy, by abandoning avant-garde music fairly early and concentrating his recording career on the classical canon. At the same time, and this is the other hand finally attacking, he was an ardent and relentless advocate of progress in the technology of mechanical reproduction. This advocacy included everything from his dismissal of concerts and critics to his championing of elaborate studio recording, new instruments, and the active role of the listener as a collaborator in musical experience.

Some of the debates on these matters must seem musty to a new-millennium audience, so it is worth pausing to consider what might be called the standard view against which Gould's stance seems so paradoxical. By the last decades of the twentieth century it had become clear that the modernist impulse in music, unlike analogous impulses in visual art or literature, had failed to alter its general landscape. Whereas non-representational art and experimental writing had by and large been accommodated, if not domesticated, by mainstream culture, such that a modernist visual aesthetic might now be found in a banker's living room and telegraphic compression (if not poetry) in his emails, the same could not be said for music.

A small coterie of enthusiasts still pursued what is sometimes called "new classical music," but in large measure the audience for music had simply shattered into atavistic regard for the canon, on one side, and those with utterly no interest in it, on the other. The first group went to concerts with orchestras and conductors to hear music mostly composed before 1900. The second group went to concerts with guitars, drums, and amplifiers to hear music mostly composed within the last ten, if not five or two, years. Innovations within the tradition of music were a lost middle term, a status they still endure.

Accounts of this linked development vary, but the standard view has it that recording technology played a large and pernicious role. "The mechanization and mass reproduction of music provided it with the means of its antimodern historical evolution," as Leon Botstein put it. The musical audience evolved in a mutation, becoming divorced from the production of music, and hence from musical literacy, because it no longer needed to acquire skills, or even travel distances, to experience music. Musically illiterate, they were also isolated, anti-social, and alienated, listening to their music alone in living rooms or automobiles—nowadays we would add, on earbuds, everywhere, all the time. Where once music brought us together, now it drove us apart, and the villain was recording technology. This "dehumanization" of the audience was but one consequence of "an extensive commercial network of music based on advanced capitalism." It likewise followed that, the machine being master, musical performance itself became a matter of rote learning, soulless repetition, synthesization, and in the most haunting example, the reduction of performance to mechanical speed and technique: the robot player.[95]

This articulation of what I have called the standard view was written in 1980. Few people would be prepared to embrace every element of the complaint—even at the time, Botstein's runaway logic and looming Skynet Terminator fears were exaggerated. Nevertheless, there is enough plausibility in the picture to show why versions of this position held then, and to some extent still do. And of course this counter-narrative of general cultural degeneration is the precise obverse of the tortured narrative of musical progress that, in elite circles at least, caught up Schoenberg and Boulez (and Stockhausen and Cage too) in its mandibles. The post-1945 story is one where even as fashion writ small is celebrating one (classical) musical innovator only to then discard him, fashion writ large is rendering the very idea of (classical) music a vestigial property, a cultural afterthought.[96]

Gould was poised uneasily in these movements. An unabashed celebrant of technology, he was also a supreme practitioner, with an intimate, almost obsessive relationship to his piano and to the history of music. His playing was technically outstanding but never mechanical—even the blistering 1955 *Goldberg Variations* was a marvel of expressive thought in action. He was progressive and anti-progressive at once, and likewise at once both a critic of the *Zeitgeist* and its most interesting expression. He was, in effect, stranded on a beachhead of his own thinking between past and future. That he was not able, by himself, to fashion a bridge between them is neither surprising nor, in the end, disappointing. We should see this failure, rather, as an aspect of his genius. He both was and was not a man of his time.

Since his death, narratives of progress have in general gone out of fashion (whether this is merely fashion is a question we are not yet in a position to say). In 1979, a year before Botstein voiced his complaint, three years before Glenn Gould's death, the philosopher and literary theorist Jean-François Lyotard, in a report written for the *Conseil des universités du Québec,* had defined the postmodern condition as one of "incredulity towards metanarratives," signalling—at least in the view of many—the end of the Enlightenment fiction of universal reason working itself out by means of history.[97] No longer could we take seriously the idea that thought moved along a smooth arc of improvement. In the art world, where the term *postmodern* had originated, this was already obvious in what the art critic Arthur Danto has called "the post-historical perspective." Once anything (any thing but also any nonthing) can be art, art is freed from a historical logic of succession and improvement. The narrative arc collapses, leaving everything—representation, abstraction, concept, performance—up for grabs.[98]

And yet, we should not assume, in our anything-goes new-millennium smugness, that such debates are now resolved. Struggles about the role of technology in music-making continue, as do even more tortuous debates about sampling, assimilation, allusions, and authenticity. Bumper stickers visible in Southern California just a few years ago claimed that "Drum Machines Have No Soul," articulating a sentiment that still longs for the human element as central to music. But the claim is not at all obvious, or definitive, since all music (save singing) depends on the intermediation of some form of *techné* or instrument. The musician and critic Franklin Bruno has noted that the only appropriate response to this bumper sticker must be "Neither Do Drum Kits."

These circumstances of confusion and contradiction are, no doubt, a function of what Botstein called a musical network structured by advanced capitalism. But there is no simple vector of succession and obsolescence even in capital and its most obedient servant, technology. As Marx noted long ago, many modes of production may co-exist in society at once, antagonistic and contradictory. Or, in McLuhan's formulation, technologies nest and wrap; they do not neatly synthesize, eliminating the prior moment.

Art is over.

CHAPTER EIGHTEEN

Art

Long live art.

As we have already seen, Gould, like most outspoken artists, had a theory about the end of art. This is firmly in the modernist tradition: it is almost as though declaring art over, or nearly so, is the necessary condition of engaging in it in the first place. Art has this in common with philosophy, that discipline of forever-declared endings. But we must distinguish Gould's version of the thesis from the generalized view that progress in art, or anyway the idea of progress in art, has come to an end.

The first important dimension of his declaration is that it is entangled in the wiring of recording technology. "I do believe that once introduced into the circuitry of art, the technological presence must be encoded and decoded," he wrote in 1975, "in such a way that its presence is, in every respect, at the service of that spiritual good that ultimately will serve to banish art itself."[99] Gould seemed to mean something like this: when technology's presence in art has finally been accepted, its ongoing negotiation will be the subject of art. And then any atavistic or magical qualities associated with the art, the sort of forbidding aura that clings to craftsmanship, mysterious genius, and visionary erudition, will be exposed as so much cliché. An educated audience will no longer be able to take seriously the old idea of art, and so that idea will consequently wither.

In places, Gould had a moralistic version of these claims. He despised ornament, like any good modernist: it is unforgivable falseness, even as recorded music, in his view, is not just forgivable but demands falsehood. (He ought to have been clearer: according to his own arguments, it was not a falsehood at all.) If Jonathan Cott's recorded phone conversations are indicative, Gould's late conversations were full of casual use of words such as "outraged," "garbage," "foolish," and—his evident favourite— "appalled" and "appalling." (Apparently they were also, less charmingly, peppered with random declines into the voices of his various personae.) Precisely what appalled him is wide in range, naturally, but it tends to involve meretriciousness or falsity in presentation, as in the case of the Beatles, or sententiousness in argument, as in those who claimed to find Muzak a scourge. From this vantage, art's end is a liberation from pretension and mystification, the ultimate democratic revolution.

But ornament is not the same as mediation. In other places, the argument invokes a somewhat woolly version of sociobiology. Contrary to standard views that technology distances us harmfully from visceral human realities such as violence or the provision of food, Gould affirmed the moral value of moving away from our more brutal selves. It follows that technology, which allows humans to do that, presents us with a clear positive choice. "Morality, it seems to me, has never been on the side of the carnivore—at least not when alternative life-styles are available," he wrote. "The evolution of man in response to his technology . . . has been anticarnivorous to the extent that, step by step, it has enabled him to operate at increasing distance from . . . his animal response to confrontation."[100] Recording technology is either an example of this moral evolution or a metaphor for it—the argument is unclear—but in any event it ought to be embraced without reservation.

It may not be obvious how art is implicated in a general sense here, but Gould asserted it this way: the "intrusion" of technology "imposes upon art a notion of morality which transcends the idea of art." Art is over when we realize the moral imperative to surrender our carnivorous attachment to the visceral, the immediate, the natural. But Gould was no decadent aesthete, celebrating artifice over nature in the manner of Oscar Wilde or Joris-Karl Huysmans's Des Esseintes. He was, instead, suggesting the inescapability, and hence the value, of intermediation. In a sense, the art/nature dichotomy disappears here, and so art ends not because playing does but because it no longer claims any special status as *either* higher or lower than nature.

The most sustained discussion Gould offered on this complex of recording, morality, and art comes in a long 1966 essay published in *High Fidelity* called "The Prospects of Recording." As ever, it is a rhetorical roller-coaster ride, with flats of clear argument disrupted by sudden mounting ascents and vertiginous polemic plunges. The last paragraph in particular is worth quoting in full: "In the best of all possible worlds, art would be unnecessary. Its offer of restorative, placative therapy would go begging a patient. The professional specialization involved in its making would be presumption. The generalities of its applicability would be an affront. The audience would be the artist and their life would be art."[101]

Parsing this knuckleball of opinion and assertion is no small task. One might see at its end a Nietzschean injunction to make one's life a work of art. Or it might be offered as a sort of aesthetic theodicy, with the deliberate echo of Wolff and Leibniz at the beginning. It could even be read as its own mini-manifesto, excoriating art-as-therapy, art-as-craft, and art-as-truth in one fell swoop, nullifying the necromantic distance between artist and audience.

But an even better question than *What does it mean?* is *Did Gould mean it?* I think yes and no. He was sincerely committed to recording technology as its own complex instrument in the world of music, and was surely correct that if music's business is reaching an audience, the means with the widest spread is best. But it is hard to believe that he really held the audience in the esteem suggested here, despite his claims that a hi-fi listener is a kind of co-creator. As he himself said more than once, the average music fan knows no more about music than an avid driver knows about the internal combustion engine. Specialization does not wither, not at least if we want to go on getting music that moves us.

Which leaves placation and generality. One need not be anti-art to reject the jejune notion that art heals. Sometimes it may, sometimes it may not; in no case is that its reason for being. On the last point, I suppose one may well feel affronted by a given artwork's claim to general applicability, but considering art in such a fashion is already a mistake. Not a moral one, an aesthetic one. Art begins to look, in Gould's formulation, suspiciously like a straw man. Who really thinks of art in these brutally reductive terms? As so often, art's declared ending is artful, part of the player's play.

CHAPTER NINETEEN

Personae

The various Goulds began to proliferate and multiply even before the fact of death brought an end to his performance of self, drawing a line beneath the score that opens the door to interpretation. Variations were being played before the piece was fully composed.

Gould displayed an evident fondness for multiple voices and characters, a persistent need to assume accents and characters for the amusement of . . . well, some would say his co-producers in the recording studio, but at this distance it is difficult to imagine anyone being fetched by these self-indulgent japes except their creator. Nor did that creator confine them to his imagination or his off-mike moments. In 1980 Columbia released the *Silver Jubilee Album*, mentioned earlier, almost one-half of which is an extended and rather strained joke radio show, *Critics Call-Out Corner*, in which Gould confronts four critics, three of them played by himself (the fourth is rendered by co-host Margaret Pacsu, who should have known better). Gould also plays the off-set sound engineer, Duncan Haig-Guinness, with a schoolyard-quality Scottish accent of the sort that is inexplicably funny to some audiences and so has somehow fuelled certain comic careers.[102]

The result is an unclassifiable piece of barely tolerable comedy that nevertheless strains to touch on various Gould preoccupations: the art of recording, the perils of performance, piano over harpsichord in interpreting Bach, and so on. The main action is run by means of a disagreement between two main characters. The liner notes explain that crusty Sir Nigel Twitt-Thornwaite has been described by *The Guardian* as exemplifying "all that is most typical in English musical life," his knighthood deriving from military as much as musical achievement. "He was cited in the New Year's List of 1941 for the courage and coordination exemplified by his rendition of Handel's 'Water Music' from the decks of the evacuation flotilla at Dunkirk in the preceding year." Opposing Sir Nigel is Professor Karlheinz Klopweisser, who has already appeared in these pages. He, for his part, has been described by *Stern* magazine as "personifying the musical equivalent of the German post-war industrial miracle," including a distinguished war record during which he created the composition "Ein Panzersymphonie" while serving with Rommel's Afrika Korps, a piece "given its world premiere at El Alamein on the evening of October 22, 1942." We learn he is "currently at work on an analysis of Glenn Gould's *Solitude Trilogy* which will be published in America under the title *Thematisch-systematisches Verzeichnis der Einsamkeit Trilogie von Glenn Gould*."

Gould—we should say, the Gould character within the fictional frame—was evidently nervous. He admitted he had soaked his hands in ice water before the recording, just as he did before performing on the piano—a clear instance of displaced anxiety ritual. And in the piece's only actually funny exchange, the Gould character is asked whether he is ready to proceed. "Well, I've just taken a Valium, Margaret," he replied with an audible smile, "and I'm trying to be as calm as one can be when confronted by a bevy of critics."[103]

Listeners will wish they were similarly fortified. With Sir Nigel tutting and harrumphing and Professor Klopweisser pontificating to Gould's murmured approval, we limp through a series of arguments about interpretation. The final Gould character, Theodore Slutz, arrives late. He is described as the Fine Arts Editor of the New York *Village Grass Is Greener*—"Equally at home with literature, painting, music and architecture, he represents a new high in the democratization of American intellectual life"—and as author of an essay collection, *Vacuum,* which provides "a unique summing-up of the state of American culture in the last decades of the twentieth century." Slutz, supposedly based on a New York cab driver Gould liked to imitate, in fact sounds like a mumbling beatnik poetaster, sprinkling liberal instances of "'man,'" "like," "you know," "dig," and "cats" in his discourse.[104]

In a final indignity, all three plus Pacsu's Hungarian Communist harridan, Marta Nortavanyi, are depicted in photographs within the gatefold album. Yes, Glenn Gould poses for the camera in various wigs and moustaches, swapping frock coat for leather jacket as the character demands. I am not making this up.

It's not that this "Glenn Gould Fantasy," as the album dubs it, has no points of interest. Gould and Klopweisser argue convincingly that one should feel free to play Gibbons on the harpsichord even though the instrument was unknown to the Tudor composer. The reason for this liberality, sometimes condemned by purists, is that they conceive music as, above all, the play of ideas rather than of notes as such. Gould's "infuriating inconsistencies" and interpretive liberties in tempo are set against the sort of "conceptual fuss and bother" that leads to a restrictive and probably incoherent "authenticity." The artist, Klopweisser argues, is "creating a point of view" with energy directed negatively, or antithetically, across the composer's impulse. "If you do it well," Gould interjects, "the end result is a far more intense and accurate realization of the original concept."

And so another version of the apologia for the 1964 withdrawal. Mere repetition in the concert setting "afflicted" the musician with a "syndrome" that led to "the slow death of the spirit." If the performance on night one was successful, the rest could only be failure instead of silence as one performed the same piece again and again. "It was a kind of torture because it ran directly counter to the spirit of invention that that first night had represented." It is worth noting that this objection is distinct from, and incompatible with, the oft-quoted non-take-twoness objection.

At this point the various voices engage in elaborately layered cross-talk, drowning one another out as they argue about whether humans can pick up multiple auditory vectors. We are then given a long account, in hockey-announcer style, of Gould's "hysteric return" performance—that is, of pieces by Tchaikovsky, Rachmaninoff, Chopin, delivered from drilling platform XP-67 in the Arctic, using one dozen pianos, to howling wind accompaniment, for the board of Geyser Petroleum. Against the background of midnight sun over the Beaufort Sea, the accompanying orchestra is stationed two miles downstream of the platform on the Canadian submarine

Inextinguishable, the production broadcast from its conning tower. Gould, sneezing and coughing, blowing his nose, eventually plays some Ravel from his knees, the famous folding chair having been carried off by a wind gust. This work is called representative of "Mr. Gould's predilection for the romantic and impressionistic repertoire," at which point the audience abruptly departs and, this being no longer a public event and therefore of no interest, the transmission must cease. Seal cries are heard as Gould mumbles, Elvis-style, "Thank you, thank you very much."

I am not making this up either. The critic Jed Distler has said of this disc, "The humor is stilted, contrived, and interesting only to true believers."[105] He was being charitable. The humour is punishing, reminiscent of a Monty Python sketch gone badly wrong or of the least tolerable of stagey early-Beatles kookiness. There can be no excuse for it, and the one clear lesson of the recording is that it could exist only because of the stature of its creator. Gould in effect called in twenty-five years of chits from Columbia when he got them to release this embarrassing piece of twaddle. Ultimately, though, it says more about Gould than about them.

Gould had played with characters before. In 1965 he published in *Musical America* several articles written by one

Dr. Herbert von Hochmeister, "distinguished Canadian scholar and critic" and "the widely read fine arts critic of *The Great Slave Smelt,* perhaps the most respected journal north of latitude 70 degrees." These arch, overwritten pieces—about the CBC, the cult of the conductor, and government patronage of the arts—are not without bite: "The very words 'Canadian Broadcast System', wafted into the night air with the soporific white-noise comfort of a staff announcer confirming a station break, bring a catch to all loyal, and liberal, throats, a tremor to all tractionless spines, a welcome certainty that what we've just heard has been stamped culturally fit."[106]

In 1968, as liner notes to his Columbia recording of Liszt's piano transcription of the Fifth Symphony by Beethoven, he offered "four imaginary reviews" by characters we can view as warmups to the 1980 piece: Sir Humphrey Price-Davies (snooty conductor), Prof. Dr. Karlheinz Heinkel (austere dialectician), S.F. Lemming, MD (reductive Freudian), and Zoltan Mostanyi (doctrinaire Communist). Despite their obviousness, these characters hold interest more than does the "fictionalized documentary for radio" from 1967, *Conference at Chillkoot,* which features keynote speaker Sir Norman Bullock-Carver, critic Homer Sibelius, avant-garde composer Alain Pauvre, and others. (The text was published by *Piano Quarterly* in 1974.)

Gould's liner notes were often brilliant, from the youthful abstractions of his first *Goldberg Variations* to the wit of the Gibbons/Byrd disc and the considered judgments of his album of Hindemith piano sonatas, for which he won an album notes Grammy in 1974—the only Grammy awarded during his lifetime. (Two posthumous ones, for best classical album and best solo performance, went to the 1982 *Variations;* his final recording, the Beethoven Piano Sonatas nos. 12 and 13, got the best solo nod in 1984.) But the belaboured humour of the imaginary reviews is best left at the dinner table, if anywhere. Unfortunately, Gould lacked such a mundane outlet even as he had access to more public ones. His fractured ideas are communicated by fractured personalities, and the numerous characters allowed him the same liberties enacted by the *High Fidelity* self-interview of 1976, only now multiplied and intended as comical. There, irony was in fact operating, if delivered with sometimes ham-handed force; here, irony has given way to self-gratification and, hence, discomfiture. We do not know where to look.

One is reminded of the peculiar unease that attends the telling of jokes in social situations, where the person being told the joke is a sort of prisoner of the person telling it. And if the joke is bad, or suggests some sort of "grasp of essential relevance," as one philosopher has defined sanity, then the unease redoubles.[107] We listen to this fantasy recording of 1980 with a growing desperate wish to make it all stop, gazing longingly at some far corner of the room.

At the root of such low-level anxiety is not the thought that Glenn Gould, lost somewhere in the bowels of Columbia's New York recording complex, had actually gone mad. It is, rather, the growing awareness that, toward the end of his life, Gould was no longer willing to maintain the fiction of a single narrative self. Instead he enjoyed the peculiar play of multiple selves that is short of fractured identity but some fairly long toss past what most of us would allow ourselves to perform in front of other people, at least while sober. Glenn Gould is having a party in his own head. Everybody is invited, but he is the only person who gets to play.

Striking, in this connection, is an ostensibly stray remark from an article he wrote about fellow Columbia Records breadwinner Barbra Streisand for *High Fidelity* in May 1976, the same year as the self-interview, comparing her to Elisabeth Schwarzkopf. After some overwrought analysis of the diva of boystown, then at her professional peak—to mention just her films, 1976 was the year of *A Star Is Born,* following *Funny Girl* in 1968, *The Owl and the Pussycat* in

1970, *What's Up, Doc?* in 1972, and *The Way We Were* in 1973—Gould revealed the following cunning thought:

> My private fantasy about Streisand is that all her greatest cuts result from dressing-room runthroughs in which (presumably to the accompaniment of a prerecorded orchestral mix) Streisand puts on one persona after another, tries out probable throwaway lines, mugs accompanying gestures to her own reflection, samples registrational couplings (super the street-urchin four-foot pipe on the sophisticated-lady sixteen-foot), and, in general, performs for her own amusement in a world of Borgean mirrors (Jorge Luis, not Victor) and word invention.[108]

Both imagery and presentation are telling here, from the self-consciously jokey reference to Borges's labyrinthine self-referential fictions (Gould could not resist the now-dated near-pun with Victor Borge) to the personification of register ranges with organ pipes and stock characters. Then there is the central conceit of imagined mirror-front mugging. This last must surely call to mind scenes of fractured selfhood: tortured adolescents, drag queens, deteriorating Norma Desmond icons, even, nowadays, a serial killer's preening psychosis. Here we confront the odd coincidence that Thomas Harris's fictional killer Hannibal Lecter has a fondness for Gould's 1955 *Goldberg Variations*. In film adaptations of the novels the music plays—albeit anachronistically—while the young Lecter injects himself with sodium thiopental as a medical student in 1951; it is also heard while the mature Lecter is mutilating a prison guard's face as part of a later escape plan.

The serious part of Gould's "private fantasy"—itself a phrase straight out of the adult-bookstore lexicon—is that which also concerns himself: namely, that the most interesting results in art may derive from a play of personae rather than the disciplined deployment of some unified aesthetic standpoint. The central irony of art would then be that unity is an emergent property rather than a precondition, an enacted but not intended distillate of crazy multiplicity.

From many takes, one recording. From many voices, one speaking. From many personae, one person.

Even more plausible is that, like Elvis Presley or Howard Hughes, Gould was lost inside the mirror-house of his own images, a prisoner of sprawling self-conception. Or that, like James Dean or Bobby Fischer, his fracturing was a function of the nascent late-century mediascape, an incandescent talent burning brightly and then out under the harsh light of public fascination. Perhaps we must say that Gould enacts elements of all these sick mini-narratives—the talent and paranoia of Fischer, the dark beauty of Dean, the creepy withdrawal of Hughes, the tortured self-medication of Presley? In any event, it is clear that he joins them as one of the first clear casualties of postmodern life, shattered remains of the cult of celebrity hastened by the very technology that made his success possible.[109]

CHAPTER TWENTY

Wonder

But, but—there is only one voice, not many, in the playing. The playing is not fractured and the playing is, finally, the thing.

Gould lived not only in his music, but as his music. The busloads of Japanese pilgrims, the academic conferences, the panel discussions, the mounting scholarly paper trail, the coffee-table books, films, commemorative stamps, devotional tattoos, and a bull market in personal relics—the whole apparatus of Gould's cult of personality, his posthumous iconic existence—amount to nothing except a puzzle. And that puzzle is, How did a performer of other people's music, however brilliant, a person who in another era would have been considered little better than a court hostler or an able cook, achieve a status of almost mythic dimensions?

The eccentricities always helped. They were the signs of Gould's exchangeable identity, the tics and tropes of talent, if not genius. We recognize them instantly, and so they constituted a large part of the assumed identity of Gould as it passed from hand to cultural hand. Humming, hunching, finicking, bundling up. Gloves and scarf and cap. Voices in the head. Seclusion, isolation, hermitage. Later, as we learn more, hypochondria, complaints, phantom illnesses, pharmacological free fall. The real Glenn Gould, whoever he was, is replaced by a loose assemblage of odd traits and strange behaviours. These stand in for the real person. No, we can go further than that: they *are* the person insofar as that person is thought about, wondered at, revered.

Hence these non-narrative takes on Gould, this forbearance from the resolved explanatory account. Jean-Paul Sartre, writing about Gustave Flaubert, said that the central issue in any biography of a creative mind is this one: how did this man become this great artist? But any such account one could offer for Glenn Gould would be finally in vain, because the name *Glenn Gould* is less a stable signifier of a person and more the call-sign of a blooming simulacral economy. Glenn Gould is everywhere and nowhere. He enacts the initial disappearance of self, priming the pump of this spectral transaction system, and then it acquires a growing energy of its own generation. Gould fascinates in part because he is so fascinating to so many. And it is of course beyond my power to hold the present book above this economy, in which it is inevitably implicated. There is nothing outside the text of Glenn Gould.

There is more to it even than this. To appreciate the full force of the issue, I hazard a cautious return to the idea of *the formative moment.* Cautious because we must not overestimate our ability to explain, even as we seek illumination of the life lived. So—we may first distinguish this category from that of defining moments, of which there are several. Gould noted the instant when he fell in love with the microphone, and so with recorded music, in 1950. He expressed his feelings of exaltation in solitude during the month-long sojourn in the Hamburg hotel room in 1958. He defended articulately at length, if sometimes contradictorily, his withdrawal from the concert stage in 1964. The turn to radio documentary in 1967 may be regarded as almost as significant. But he also hinted at a moment when his love for music—his peculiar version of it, I mean—was excited. The moment takes us back to Mr. Gibbons, who emerges as his kindred spirit and something like his occupying muse.

In the 1972 self-interview, Gould queried himself about his famous likes and dislikes. He expressed doubts about Beethoven and most of the later Mozart, works which he played often and recorded. To understand this, the interviewing Gould suggested a distinction, namely that "such performances simply provided you with tactile rather than intellectual stimulation." The interviewed Gould resisted this, saying he "tried very, very hard to develop a convincing rationale" for a given Beethoven performance. The operative word is *tried*, and the first Gould did not hesitate to jump on this: there is a resistance there, an argument; the rationale may have been developed, but it was a chore—uphill work. By contrast, if the second Gould were to play a piece by his favourite composer, Orlando Gibbons, "then every note would seem to belong organically without any necessity for you as its interpreter to differentiate between tactile and intellectual considerations at all." That is, there would be no need to try to rationalize, still less to *try to like*, Gibbons's "Salisbury" Pavan. And so, were the second Gould to sit down late at night, just him and CD 318 alone in his room, to play some Gibbons rather than some Beethoven, no "schizophrenic tendencies" between thought and deed would be in evidence.[110]

The self-analysis here gives way to a larger theory of musical history, just the sort of thing that Gould enjoyed sending up. Interviewed Gould cannot reject Beethoven, interviewing Gould argued, because that is to abandon a logic of historical progression that moves music more and more into an expressive mode. Post-Renaissance art "achieves its communicative power," he said, by creating a sort of tune-bath into which the listener is invited to sink. The player may massage an interpretation to his own ends, but the larger ideology cannot be evaded. And this is what the second Gould resented, and so has formed a pattern of hatred and rejection.

Of course, Gould did not reject the post-Renaissance composers at all, but this schizophrenic conversation about schizophrenic tendencies in his playing allowed him to communicate that idea even while not enacting it. He acknowledged he was not prepared to assert, as John Cage famously did, that "Beethoven was wrong!"[111] That is, he did not believe linear motivic development in music was at a dead end, in need of replacement by Zen not-quite-silences such as Cage's composition 4'33". But he did want to say, in effect, that Gibbons was right. And that rightness, properly understood, combined with the memory of a formative moment, makes for a revealing insight about Gould the thinker, Gould the musician.

Recall the memory Gould shared two years before the self-interview of the Deller Consort rendition of anthems and madrigals by Gibbons, chosen as his no-contest first choice of desert island discs. Alfred Deller, a counter-tenor who died in 1979, had formed the Consort in the years after the Second World War in order to revive and celebrate the polyphonic vocal music of the Renaissance, in particular the many pieces featuring that ethereal male range equivalent to contralto, mezzo-soprano, or soprano. This singing and its music have enjoyed a deserved vogue in the years since Deller's (and Gould's) death, but at the time Gould was growing up it was decidedly out of fashion. On this evidence alone, a teenager of 1948 or 1949 who found counter-tenor-led polyphonic Elizabethan church music the most moving thing he was ever to know would have been a very strange creature indeed.

What was it that drew Gould so profoundly to the music of Gibbons? First, I think, the felicitous combination of complex counterpoint and accessible melody: Gibbons's music has an easy grace that belies its intellectual heft. The results are structurally beautiful, rich in the congruent incongruities that please the listener—here consciousness, engaged in active pattern-recognition, is stimulated over and over again. The themes of the vocal compositions are mostly devotional, given the times, but the other works follow the conventions of dance, the pavan, galliard, and allemande styles imported to England from Italy and France. All of this combines in a small but glittering oeuvre by the leading court musician of his time, and so it exactly answers to Gould's stated preferences: clear line, contrapuntal depth, and melodic sweetness but without overbearing or predictable motives. This is music of "direct and emphatic" cadence, with "an amazing insight into the psychology of the tonal system."

But there is also a problem waiting to be solved, at least in the non-vocal works. "Gibbons is an artist of such intractable commitment that, in the keyboard field at least, his works work better in one's memory, or on paper, than they ever can through the intercession of the sounding-board."[112] In other words, there is a tension even here between the tactile and the intellectual, but one that calls out for an intercession: work still, but this time downhill work.

As we have seen, Gould the philosopher struggled, as most do, to articulate the being of music even as Gould the performer made music almost without pause. Does music lie in the mind, or in the fingers? Neither, really. Arguing with Geoffrey Payzant in his review, Gould wrote that "the mental imagery involved with pianistic tactilia is *not* related to the striking of the individual keys but rather to the rites of passage *between* notes."[113] But what lies between the notes is of course nothing, the silence of music's possibility. Negotiating that space, performing that rite of passage—what a telling phrase that is—is just where mind meets music, and vice versa. The striking of the keys is in a sense no more than a means to that end. No more, but also no less.

What a wonder, then, for a performer to find a composer whose mind is so affinitive to his own that playing his music feels exactly like making it up as he goes. And what a wonder for us to hear playing of a score that is so seamlessly inhabited that it sounds just as it feels. Unfolded in time, it somehow manages at once to surprise us and to tell us exactly what we already know. Great music, like a will in law, is self-proving: its rightness lies precisely in its demonstration and nowhere else. And yet, at the same time—in the same time—this project is never complete or ideal because it negotiates the gaps, between notes, between intellect and touch, only as it acknowledges that they cannot ever be closed.

Since ancient times, philosophers have called this experience of conjoined expansion and recognition *wonder*. Wonder is that which excites the mind without offering itself to smooth understanding under the power of a ready concept. There is, I think, no better word for the exhilarating, demanding, and self-justifying experience of encountering a Glenn Gould interpretation—even if, sometimes, he has to try very, very hard to find the line of its reasoning for us to consider.

Gould, in an optimistic mood in 1962, on the wonder of art: "The justification of art is the internal combustion it ignites in the hearts of men and not its shallow, externalized, public manifestations. The purpose of art is not the release of a momentary ejection of adrenaline but is, rather, the gradual, lifelong construction of a state of wonder and serenity."[114]

CHAPTER TWENTY-ONE

Takes

In life, as in concert performance, there is a non-take-twoness that we might well resent. We never have the benefit that the simplest recording studio confers, of doing it over one more time.

The musical take grabs a performance, pins it to the storage/retrieval technology. It is only *taken* if it can be put away in order to be taken out again and used. Played. Dictionary entries for the transitive verb *take* are among the longest to be found—perhaps indicating the number of ways and things we are concerned to take. For the noun *take*, the entry is short—the amount of type set up in a given session (archaic now); the continuous recorded scene or rendering in cinema and music; and the monies collected from a theatrical or sporting performance—and almost always accompanied by the definite article: *the* take.

The recording take reminds us, as the piece of music itself cannot, of the tension between part and whole that is the essence of music. The take records the moments of negotiation between past and future, held fitfully, contingently, in the loose frame of the present. We cannot see that frame, cannot isolate it, yet we cannot experience music or anything else without its presumptive presence. If presence is even the right word. Its functioning. Its allowance. Its grace.

Music is perception, but it is not only perception; it is also a perception of that which makes perception possible, a glimpse of the conditions making perception possible. Music is thought, but it is not cognition—it has no fixed meaning or even a determinate concept. It does not follow from this, from the non-cognitive status of music, that it is without import. On the contrary, music matters even though it does not mean. Music matters *because* it does not mean. Any anthropological or evolutionary account of music's mattering, no matter how nuanced, will not be able to account for this mattering beyond meaning. Music embraces the promise of happiness given by all beauty.[115]

Music is like conversation, or a joke, or consciousness: all are structures of anticipation and resolution, expectation and incongruity, negotiations with time. We can plot the line of music just as we might plot the structure of a joke or a conversation, but this line or structure will not *be* the joke, the conversation, the music. Perhaps it is right to say: music is consciousness. Music's play of expectation and resolution, its set-ups and punchlines, its surprising satisfactions and satisfactory surprises, are the stuff of mind itself. And like mind, a given piece of music must come to its end, must subside into silence. It must die, or die out—bang or whimper does not signify. But to die is not to perish. The performance ends but the piece lives on, to be played again. And again. Taken.

Music is not the food of love, it is the food of life. Music is eros, basic life energy, existing before parseable meaning and not reducible to it.

On October 4, 1982, at the decision of his father, the systems supporting the life of Glenn Gould—the bodily life, at least; perhaps not the consciousness he never recovered—were withdrawn. He was buried in Mount Pleasant Cemetery next to his mother; his father, having suffered the tragedy of outliving a child, would later join them there. On Glenn's marker there is carved a piano, as well as the first two and a half bars of the aria from the *Goldberg Variations*.

A person is not one thing. A person is a composition improvised by the maker. We each can try to play it.

Start again. Da capo. From the top.

[1] Geoffrey Payzant, in his *Glenn Gould, Music and Mind* (Toronto: Key Porter, 1978; rev. ed. 1984) will note the relation in reverse, namely that "Gould displays astonishing control over these consonants [of individual musical notes] in his piano playing (just as he does, incidentally, in his speech)" (p. 117).

[2] My transcription from the audio disc *Glenn Gould: Concert Dropout* (Columbia BS15, 1968).

[3] Ian McEwan, *Saturday* (New York: Knopf, 2005), p. 5. The narrator is noting the depression the main character, a London neurosurgeon called Henry Perowne, feels while reading a biography of Charles Darwin in order to please his literary daughter. This same neurosurgeon likes to play piano recordings of Bach while in the operating theatre. "He favours Angela Hewitt, Martha Argerich, sometimes Gustav Leonhardt. In a really good mood he'll go for the looser interpretations of Glenn Gould" (p. 21). Later, considering his four recorded versions of the *Goldberg Variations,* Perowne "selects not the showy unorthodoxies of Glenn Gould, but Angela Hewitt's wise and silky playing which includes all the repeats" (p. 257).

A commentator has noted that this reference indicates Gould's 1955 debut, "which is notable for its unorthodox tempos and for ignoring the 'A' section repeats" in the canons, the Fughetta, and the other fugue-like elements. This interpretation is looser in intellectual, not technical, terms; and that only arguably. Hewitt's deliberately paced *Goldberg,* at 78 minutes, 32 seconds, is almost a half-hour longer than Gould's 1981 version—that is, the slow Gould, which clocks in at 51 minutes, 18 seconds (the 1955 record is just 38 minutes, 34 seconds long). Hewitt, the recent Canadian star with a special genius for precise but emotional renderings of Bach—some find them overfond of rubato—has grown understandably weary of comparisons to Gould, whom she remembers seeing on Canadian television and thinking rather strange.

[4] Tim Page, ed., *The Glenn Gould Reader* (Toronto: Key Porter, 1984), p. 438. [Hereafter *GGR*.]

[5] My transcription from the liner notes; also *GGR*, p. 11.

[6] Jerrold Levinson, *Music in the Moment* (1997; rev. ed. Ithaca: Cornell University Press, 2007), offers an accessible philosophical engagement with this problem.

[7] BWV988, first published in 1741.

[8] *GGR*, p. 23.

[9] Reprinted in the liner notes to a reissue of the 1955 *Goldberg Variations* (Columbia MS7096); quoted in Payzant, *Glenn Gould*, p. 15. This chair can be heard creaking in most of the recordings of Gould's career and so becomes, as Payzant notes, "as much a secondary trademark of his performance as his vocal noise" (p. 77).

[10] My transcription from the liner notes; also *GGR*, p. 28.

[11] CBC Radio broadcast (April 30, 1967); quoted in Payzant, *Glenn Gould*, p. 37.

[12] The art of interpretation is situated, on Gould's own understanding of it, in critical, improvisational, and multilayered territory. There is

no single correct interpretation of a piece, only a host of choices and references; as a result, any given musical interpretation speaks of and to the world at large, not just of and to the musical score. Gould's writing shows the same range and complexity, the same serious playfulness. We could therefore say that he is more a *hermenaut* than a *hermeneut,* and conclude that we must incline ourselves likewise if we are to recite the score of his life. (My thanks to Joshua Glenn for clarification of this point.)

[13] A fictional one, as it happens: the narrator of Christopher Miller's Gould-inflected novel, *Simon Silber: Works for Solo Piano* (New York: Houghton Mifflin Harcourt, 2002); see note 18.

[14] For those so inclined, this is a crude way of characterizing the difference between Sartrean existential alienation (the other as presumptive accuser or threat) and the existential recognition found in Levinas (other-being as forever calling me to ethical account).

[15] Dennis Braithwaite, "Glenn Gould," *Toronto Daily Star* (March 28, 1959); quoted in Payzant, *Glenn Gould,* p. 3.

[16] See, e.g., Paul Ricoeur, *Oneself As Another* (English trans. Kathleen Blamey, Chicago: University of Chicago Press, 1995).

[17] Slavoj Žižek, *Looking Awry: An Introduction to Jacques Lacan Through Popular Culture* (Cambridge, Mass.: MIT Press, 1991), p. 69.

[18] Miller's *Simon Silber* is sometimes included as a fictional treatment of a Gould-like pianist. In fact the main character, though entertainingly eccentric, bears no resemblance to Gould and has none of his playful oddness; but there are some enlivening jokes

about the connection. The novel, a series of commissioned biographical liner notes for Silber's compositions, includes an explanation of the *"Babbage" Permutations,* a work dedicated to the mathematician Charles Babbage, inventor of the computer. Allegedly "inspired by the Schumann work, [it] is simply an exhaustive computer-generated set of permutations on the sequence 'B-A-B-B-A-G-E', played here in the evenhanded manner of Glenn Gould— whom my friend admired and resented to the end" (pp. 9–10). The narrator, an out-of-work philosophy graduate, was born on February 29, 1960, and "in off years" celebrated his birthday on March 1—my own birthday, incidentally, and not far off on the year (1963).

A more evident fictional treatment is David Young's 1992 play, *Glenn* (rev. ed. Toronto: Coach House Press, 1998), which breaks Gould's character into four alliterative facets (prodigy, performer, perfectionist, puritan) and explores the dimensions of his thought, like Girard's film, with a repeated aria and thirty variations (scenes). Gould also makes a caricature appearance (along with Josephine Baker, Fred Astaire, and Django Reinhardt) in the 2003 animated film *Les triplettes de Belleville.*

To take just two recent works by Canadian writers that feature a fictional or inspirational Gould: (1) Gould makes a cameo appearance in Jonathan Bennett's novel *Entitlement* (Toronto: misFit Books, 2008) encountered at the Fran's all-night diner on St. Clair Avenue and—somewhat implausibly—heard quoting from memory the lyrics to a Clash song. And (2), in Jeramy Dodds's poetry collection *Crabwise to the Hounds* (Toronto: Coach House Press, 2008), Gould features in four different poems: "Dictaphone reel of Glenn Gould's last gasp" (p. 53); "Modulated timbre and cadence for baby grand" (p. 57), which quotes his "resentment" of concert playing's "non-take-twoness'" as an epigraph; "Glenn Gould negotiates the Danube in the company of a raven" (pp. 63–66), a long prose poem; and "The easiest way to empty a seashell is to place it on an anthill" (pp. 48–51). The last begins, "At first his right and left hands hover over the keys / before falling to the ivory / like a luggage-bombed Boeing" and continues with a series of ever more elaborate metaphors for the attack style of the two hands: "His right skis to the North Star, seeing-eye dog of explorers. / His left pivots at the star and stumbles in perfect harmony / like an actor playing the Bullet-Riddled Man" (p. 49).

A reviewer who noted that appearances of Gould in Canadian poems are now so frequent as to amount to "a verse cliché" forgave Dodds his move only because the poet showed "the same idiosyncratic brilliance that the famed concert pianist injected into his own art." Well, maybe. In any event, a non-exhaustive list of recent poets, not all Canadian, who mention or enlist Gould in verse form would include J.D. Smith, Kate Braid, Bruce Bond, Ann LeZott, Richard M. McErlean, Jonathan Holden, and Janine Canan.

The *Goldberg Variations,* in a related movement, have themselves inspired artwork in other forms, from Nancy Huston's satirical debut novel *Les variations Goldberg* (1981; English trans. Montreal: Signature Editions, 1996), wherein one character deprecates "the frenzied charge of a Glenn Gould" attacking the piece, to a 1984 painting by Gerhard Richter, *Goldberg-Variationen,* in the shape of a long-playing vinyl disc. (I thank Angela Hewitt for the last example.)

[19] This might be considered the inverse of the standard situation, whereby someone is inspired or elevated by the same music. For example, in the ultraviolent 2008 remake of the science-fiction classic *The Day the Earth Stood Still*—popularly dubbed "The Day Keanu Reeves Stood Still"—the visiting environmental clean-up alien Klaatu (Reeves, in an exquisitely expressionless performance) is in part persuaded to spare humanity when he hears the aria da capo and Variation 1 played (out of order) by Ryan Franks. "It's beautiful," he says. A good-looking scientist (Jennifer Connelly) hugging her stepchild also gives him pause. Humanity brutally exploits the planet, yes, but we're not *all* bad.

Meanwhile, the situation whereby a musician of talent is sent into despair, perhaps suicide, by overhearing or witnessing a musician of genius is a familiar one. Versions of it can be found in Peter Shaffer's *Amadeus* (1979; New York: HarperCollins, 1981) and Rebecca West's *The Fountain Overflows* (New York: Viking, 1956). Other stories, possibly apocryphal, have the songwriter Gerry Coffin pushed into madness by the example of Bob Dylan, and guitarists Eric Clapton and Pete Townshend overpowered and shamed by a Jimi Hendrix performance. The American novelist Mark Salzman, son of a musician, planned a musical career and entered Yale at sixteen to study it; after hearing cellist Yo-Yo Ma play at Tanglewood, he gave up in despair and majored in Chinese instead—surely a common experience. The sculptor Richard Serra, in a different dynamic for which we may be thankful, allegedly gave up painting after seeing Velázquez's *Las Meninas*, despairing of bettering him.

[20] This is how Martin Amis defines alcoholism, not philosophy, in his novel *Night Train* (New York: Vintage, 1997), perhaps after the remark made by Sara Mayfield that her friend F. Scott Fitzgerald was killing himself via layaway. Procrastination has also been so defined. My version has the historical sanction of the Socratic definition of philosophy as *learning how to die*. Cf. Plato, *Phaedo* Book I: "The philosopher desires death—which the wicked world will insinuate that he also deserves: and perhaps he does, but not in any sense which they are capable of understanding. Enough of them: the real question is, What is the nature of that death which he desires? Death is the separation of soul and body—and the philosopher desires such a separation. He would like to be freed from the dominion of bodily pleasures and of the senses, which are always perturbing his mental vision. He wants to get rid of eyes and ears, and with the light of the mind only to behold the light of truth."

[21] All quotations from Bernhard, *The Loser* (1991; English trans. Jack Dawson, New York: Vintage, 2006).

[22] Oliver Sacks, *Musicophilia: Tales of Music and the Brain* (New York: Knopf, 2007).

[23] Quoted and discussed in Sacks, *Musicophilia*; quotations from Nabokov and Freud likewise. The Amis and Mann references are mine.

[24] The thought-experiment is taken from Andy Clark and David Chalmers, "The Extended Mind," *Analysis* 58 (1998): 10–23. Another vivid example: a sight-impaired man uses a cane to find

his way. It seems hard to deny that the cane is part of his (extended) mind. The resulting position in philosophy of mind is sometimes called *active externalism,* and is considered novel. But note that the basic insight can be found already in the phenomenological literature (e.g., Heidegger's discussion of the lecture hall, which exists as part of my concern before I enter it) and even in McLuhan's notion of mass media as "extensions of the sensorium." I have further discussion of this in *Concrete Reveries: Consciousness and the City* (Toronto and New York: Viking, 2008).

[25] Nor, for that matter, does McLuhan's famous distinction between hot and cool media, deployed throughout his magnum opus, *Understanding Media: The Extensions of Man* (1964; rev. ed. Cambridge, Mass.: MIT Press, 1994), hold much water. McLuhan is strongest on the shifts in larger effect that changes in media bring to societies, and cleverly shows, among other things, how housing, money, and clocks function as media in the larger sense. More arresting still is the deft cultural criticism collected in his first book of media theory, *The Mechanical Bride: Folklore of Industrial Man* (1951; rev. ed. New York: Vanguard Press, 1967), a book that Gould surely knew well. It is here that the visual space/acoustic space distinction is first mooted. For more, see Richard Cavell, *McLuhan in Space: A Cultural Geography* (Toronto: University of Toronto Press, 2002).

[26] Huston, *The Goldberg Variations,* p. 90. The thought actually belongs to the character Bernald Thorer, whose inner monologue forms "Variation XV" in Huston's thirty-two-part novel, a sequence of meditations entertained while the various characters listen to one of their number performing Bach's composition on harpsichord.

[27] MacLeish's familiar claim that "A poem should not mean / But be" is found in his poem "Ars Poetica" (1926). At first this paradoxical poem appears to flatly self-contradict: as with all *ars poetica* statements, it is a normative manifesto, an argument. Indeed, there are no less than six instances of the word *should* peppering its lines! Thus its meaning is clear and definitive; it has a thesis. But that thesis—that a poem should not mean—is overturned by the performance, indeed the very being, of the poem making that claim.

And yet, at the very same time, that thesis is also brilliantly realized, not denied, in the series of deft concrete images: of things and experiences that move us, or (we might better say) that make us suddenly still. A flight of birds; the climbing moon; ripe fruit; an old medallion. A poem should be like *that*, "palpable and mute," as it says itself. Mute? But if a poem does anything, it speaks. There it is, after all, sitting on the page (or coming from the speaker's mouth). It's as *un-mute* as almost anything we can imagine. And so it goes, idea and expression at eternal war with themselves within the special paradoxical immanence of this poem about poems, this thought about thoughts.

Logically speaking, the contradiction can be resolved with a move to deepen the meaning of *meaning*. That is, poems are evaluated incorrectly if meaning is construed narrowly as *propositional content* or *truth conditions*. They have neither, and we make a mistake if we seek them in poetry, reducing living power to distilled summaries or morals. We make an even worse mistake if, failing to find propositional content or truth value, we denigrate poetry. If the notion of meaning is expanded, on the other hand, we can speak of the meaning of a poem, not just its being or its music. Of course that meaning will remain elusive, layered, fugitive; that is part of its appeal.

[28] Daniel Levitin, *The World in Six Songs: How the Musical Brain Created Human Nature* (New York: Viking, 2008).

[29] Joe Pernice's *Meat Is Murder* (New York: Continuum, 2003), in the 33 1/3 series, is an apposite fictionalized memoir of his experience of high school in Boston when music, especially by innovative English bands, was structurally scarce. Nick Hornby's novel *High Fidelity* (New York: Riverhead, 1995) does the same in the English context of roughly the same period (early 1980s). Both make it clear how important access to music, not just choice of it, functions as a marker of personal cultural identity.

[30] See Pierre Bourdieu, *Distinction: A Social Critique of the Judgment of Taste* (1979; English trans. Richard Nice, Cambridge, Mass.: Harvard University Press, 1984). Bourdieu is well aware of potential reductionism in this kind of analysis of taste; ultimately he works to highlight what he calls the *paradox of the imposition of legitimacy*. This paradox "is what makes it impossible ever to determine whether the dominant feature appears distinguished because it is dominant—i.e., because it has the privilege of defining, by its very existence, what is noble or distinguished as being exactly what itself is, a privilege which is expressed precisely in its self-assurance—or whether it is only because it is dominant that it appears endowed with these qualities and uniquely entitled to define them" (p. 92).

[31] My transcription from the audio disc.

[32] Harold Bloom, *Genius: A Mosaic of One Hundred Exemplary Creative Minds* (New York: Grand Central Books, 2002). Bloom's choice of one hundred names, organized according to a wacky kabbalistic diagram of his own devising, is controversial, even to himself: "Aside from those who could not be omitted—Shakespeare, Dante, Cervantes, Homer, Vergil, Plato, and their peers," Bloom says in his preface, "my choice is wholly arbitrary and idiosyncratic. They are certainly *not* 'the top one hundred,' in anyone's judgment, my own included. I wanted to write about these." Bloom's chosen ones include Lewis Carroll, but not Racine or Rabelais; Walter Pater, but not Addison or Hume; Iris Murdoch, but not Nabokov; Browning, but not Marvell. Wallace Stevens, yes; Auden, no. Flannery O'Connor, Hart Crane, Willa Cather, Ralph Ellison—all here. Evelyn Waugh and Anthony Powell—absent. No then-living writers are included, so who knows about Anne Carson (conceded as probable), Saul Bellow, Thomas Pynchon, Don DeLillo, David Foster Wallace, John Updike, or Michael Ondaatje.

[33] Henry Perowne, for one. Ian McEwan's fictional neurosurgeon and Angela Hewitt fan says he cannot make sense of the notion of writing of genius. Bloom himself passes over the likes of "Einstein, Delacroix, Mozart, Louis Armstrong." Also, let it be said, Edmund Keane, W.G. Grace, Alfred Hitchcock, Fred Astaire, Curtis Mayfield, Ludwig Wittgenstein, and Wayne Gretzky. He does include Plato, the Yahwist, Saint Paul, Kierkegaard, and Freud. (For the record, in his *Fred Astaire* [New Haven: Yale University Press, 2008], Joseph Epstein considers and rejects the claim that Astaire was a genius, though he acknowledges that the dancer "was immensely, charmingly, winningly talented" [p. 185]. So much for that.)

[34] William Gass, "The Test of Time," in *Tests of Time* (Chicago: University of Chicago Press, 2002), pp. 102–26. Gass speaks in the end of the incalculable value of "the combination of occasion, consciousness, and artful composition" that makes for art. "Don't take the test," he advises. "For works of art, the rule reads: never enter Time, and you will never be required to exit" (p. 126).

[35] The distinction is so common as to arise even in popular culture. In the 1963 film *The War Lover* (based on a John Hersey novel), Robert Wagner and Steve McQueen play rival B-17 pilots both in love with the same woman (Shirley Anne Field). McQueen's character, aggressive and obsessed, steals her away from Wagner's but, in the end, attempts a dangerous manoeuvre that results in his death. Trying to explain McQueen's undeniable appeal over his own more reliable demeanour, Wagner attributes it to "the difference between talent and genius." A *New York Times* reviewer of the day was not convinced: "Altogether [the three] make what at best is an average drama of love and jealousy into a small and tepid exposition of one man's absurd cantankerousness."

[36] All quotations from Kant, *Critique of Judgment* (*Kritik der Urteilskraft*, 1790; English trans. Paul Guyer and Eric Matthews, Cambridge: Cambridge University Press, 2001). Kant considered poetry the highest of the arts, followed by representational visual art and sculpture; music he regarded as too often noisome. "The case of music is almost like that of the delight derived from a smell that diffuses itself widely," he said. "The man who pulls his perfumed handkerchief out of his pocket attracts the attention of all around him, even against their will, and he forces them, if they are

to breathe at all, to enjoy the scent; hence this habit has gone out of fashion." Well, no it hasn't, for neither music nor scent.

[37] Again for those so inclined, it is worth noting here that this cluster of concepts aligns with Gilles Deleuze's distinction between the *virtual* and the *possible/actual*. The virtual is neither possible nor actual, but instead the background concept of a range of possibilities itself; the possible is limited by its dyadic relation with the actual; it is the not-yet-actual and so, in a sense, always already determined by the actual.

[38] Giorgio Agamben, *The Coming Community* (trans. Michael Hardt; Minneapolis: University of Minnesota Press, 1993), p. 36. It is a curious omission in Agamben's otherwise nuanced text that, taking so much care analyzing the notion of *quodlibet* and explicitly mentioning Gould in this connection, he does not seem to notice the connection to Goldberg Variation 30 and its classification as a musical quodlibet.

[39] Quoted in Payzant, *Glenn Gould,* pp. 13–14.

[40] Quoted in Kevin Bazzana, *Wondrous Strange: The Life and Art of Glenn Gould* (Toronto: McClelland & Stewart, 2004), pp. 170–71; and Otto Friedrich, *Glenn Gould: A Life and Variations* (1989; rev. ed. Toronto: Key Porter Books, 2002), p. 153.

[41] Quoted in Bazzana, *Wondrous Strange,* p. 172; Peter Ostwald, *Glenn Gould: The Ecstasy and Tragedy of Genius* (New York: W.W. Norton, 1997), pp. 155–56; and mentioned in Payzant, *Glenn Gould,* p. 17.

[42] Jonathan Cott, *Conversations with Glenn Gould* (1984; rev. ed. Chicago: University of Chicago Press, 2005), p. 106.

[43] Maurice Natanson, *The Erotic Bird: Phenomenology in Literature* (1998; rev. ed. Princeton: Princeton University Press, 2004), pp. 87, 90, 92. I am grateful for the experience of knowing and working as a teaching assistant to Natanson in the Yale College literature and philosophy class that informs this wise and brilliant book, the last he completed before his death in 1996.

[44] Slavoj Žižek, "Notes towards a politics of Bartleby: The ignorance of chicken," *Comparative American Studies* 4 (2006): 375–94, at p. 381; reprinted in Žižek, *The Parallax View* (Cambridge, Mass.: MIT Press, 2006), ch. 6. Elizabeth Hardwick, "Bartleby in Manhattan," in *American Fictions* (New York: Modern Library, 1999), p. 8; the essay was first published in 1981.

There are of course multiple Bartlebys, even speaking only politically; Armin Beverungen and Stephen Dunne, in "'I'd Prefer Not To': Bartleby and the Excesses of Interpretation," *Culture and Organization* 13, no. 2 (June 2007): 171–83, suggest that this interpretive fecundity is itself a site of *textual* surplus or excess. The story generates an ungraspable and always unresolved remainder not exhausted by Antonio Negri, Michael Hardt, and Žižek's "political" Bartleby, Gilles Deleuze's "originary" Bartleby, or Agamben's "whatever" Bartleby. "On the basis of these interpretations we derive a concept of excess as the residual surplus of any categorical interpretation, the yet to be accounted for, the not yet explained, the un-interpretable, the indeterminate, the always yet to arrive, precisely that which cannot be captured, held onto or put in place" (p. 171).

The character Bartleby refuses to be assimilated within the story; the philosopheme "Bartleby" likewise refuses to submit completely to any single interpretive assignment or form of consumption! For more on this issue and its relation to political critique, see Mark Kingwell, "Masters of Chancery: The Gift of Public Space," in Kingwell and Patrick Turmel, eds., *Rites of Way: The Politics and Poetics of Public Space* (Kitchener-Waterloo: Wilfrid Laurier University Press, 2009).

[45] Agamben, *The Coming Community,* p. 36.

[46] My transcription from the audio disc *Glenn Gould: Concert Dropout.*

[47] My transcription from the audio disc *Glenn Gould: Concert Dropout.*

[48] Jarrett hums and moans, sometimes sings wordlessly, at various moments in his astonishing free-form concert in Köln, Germany, in 1975. Later studio recordings of jazz standards, done in 1983 with Gary Peacock and Jack DeJohnette—a trio still recording and performing together a quarter-century later—feature even more marked vocalizing, sometimes to the point of irritating the listener (well, this listener). Cf. *Setting Standards: New York Sessions* (New York: ECM, 2008), the multiple-disc reissue of the original releases from 1984 and 1985.

Jarrett has not recorded a great deal of classical music, but he has released some Bach performances, and his version of the *Goldberg Variations* offers yet another distinct interpretive argument for that great work. His choice of harpsichord rather than piano is curious, if historically accurate, and makes for a somewhat churchy (or maybe lair-of-the-evil-genius) rendering—what Gould would disparage as the "sewing-machine" effect.

[49] *GGR,* pp. 35–36.

[50] I can certainly recall the baffled rage that erupted at a 1979 Toronto concert by the British pop group Queen, who walked off the stage during a playback of their monster hit "Bohemian Rhapsody"—they wouldn't even pretend to realize its overwrought lushness live. In a different but related category are those artists who are reviled as frauds for either (1) not singing on their own recordings (e.g., the dreadlocked 1980s duo Milli Vanilli, exposed as gyrating mannequins fronting other people's voices) or (2) trying to pass off a recorded performance of their singing as a live one (e.g., Ashlee Simpson appearing on the television show *Saturday Night Live* and having her lip-sync routine spoiled by a technical glitch).

[51] Of course this is just the barest beginning in Kant's *a priori* investigation of human knowledge in *The Critique of Pure Reason* (*Kritik der reinen Vernunft*, 1781; English trans. Werner Pluhar and Patricia Kitcher, New York: Hackett, 1996). There must also be "categories of understanding" (twelve in total, broken under the four headings of quantity, quality, relation, and modality) and the so-called ideas of reason (self, universe, God), not to mention the resolution of various antinomies via analytic reasoning.

[52] *GGR*, p. 92; the immediate context is a 1962 *High Fidelity* essay in praise of Richard Strauss.

[53] See Henri Lefebvre, *The Production of Space* (English trans. Hoboken: Wiley-Blackwell, 1991). Lefebvre's expansive "critique of everyday life" includes reflections on music, architecture, and the relation between them under the sign of consciousness and the city.

[54] *GGR*, p. 237.

[55] My transcription from the liner notes; also *GGR,* p. 13.

[56] Quoted and discussed in Alfred Schutz, *Collected Papers,* vol. 2: *Studies in Social Theory* (Berlin: Springer Verlag, 1964), p. 199.

[57] Johan Huizinga, *Homo Ludens: A Study of the Play Element in Culture* (1944; English trans. 1950; rev. ed. Boston: Beacon Press, 1971); quotations from pp. ix, 3, 6, and 11.

[58] Stephen Potter's deadpan satires on this topic are instructive. In *Gamesmanship* (London: Rupert Hart-Davis, 1947), *Lifemanship* (London: Rupert Hart-Davis, 1950), *One-Upmanship* (London: Rupert Hart-Davis, 1952), and *Supermanship* (New York: Random House, 1958), he provides all the essential tactics for true gamesmanship, which is the art of being one up by putting the other fellow one down.

[59] See James P. Carse, *Finite and Infinite Games* (New York: Ballantine Books, 1987). Carse views the distinction negatively: finite games, preoccupied with winning and finishing, dominate in life as well as sports; infinite games are, for him, revelatory of deeper human possibilities. Carse has larger metaphysical ambitions, not always so well judged. For example, he solves the genius question in the book's third section, "I Am the Genius of Myself," by claiming that each one of us is, well, the genius of him- or herself. There you go.

[60] For more, see Huizinga, *Homo Ludens,* ch. 10; also Mark Kingwell and Joshua Glenn, *The Idler's Glossary* (Emeryville: Biblioasis, 2008). To be sure, the standard Greek view at the time of Aristotle was that music was straightforwardly useful, a form of moral education.

[61] Gould's love affair with this instrument—"It's quite extraordinary, it has a clarity of every register that I think is just about unique. I adore it," he told Jonathan Cott (*Conversations*, p. 47)—has been well documented by himself in various liner notes and interviews, and discussed ably by Katie Hafner in *A Romance on Three Legs: Glenn Gould's Obsessive Quest for the Perfect Piano* (New York: Bloomsbury, 2008); see also the crisp discussion in Payzant, *Glenn Gould*, pp. 104–108.

[62] http://wiki.answers.com/Q/What_famous_people_have_Asperger's_Syndrome

[63] If one includes fictional characters who might have Asperger syndrome, the list welcomes, among others, Bert from *Sesame Street* (not Ernie), Lisa Simpson, Calvin (of *Calvin and Hobbes*), Dilbert (of *Dilbert*), Pippi Longstocking, Sherlock Holmes, Hercule Poirot, Chauncey Gardiner from Jerzy Kosinski's *Being There*, Ignatius Reilly from John Kennedy Toole's *A Confederacy of Dunces,* and—yes—who could forget the poster boy for social withdrawal, Bartleby the Scrivener. Alert readers will notice that the title of Toole's novel is itself a reference to Swift's dry version of how we may spot the genius.

And in case none of this is convincing, note how one possible Asperger case, Gould, is drawn repeatedly to the imagery of another, Schulz: in a liner note from 1973 the pianist notes that "as his career came to a close, Hindemith drew consistency around him like a Linus blanket" (*GGR*, p. 148). Then, in a 1974 *Piano Quarterly* article about the eccentric musician Ernst Krenek, Gould mentions how he goes outside only after "mobilizing my backup scarf as a Linus blanket" (*GGR*, p. 189). Coincidence?

[64] Alfred Bester, "The Zany Genius of Glenn Gould," *Holiday* 35, no. 4 (April 1964), p. 153; quoted in Payzant, *Glenn Gould,* p. 95. "Here reason tottered," Bester had commented at the time, but philosopher Payzant is more astute. He knows that Gould is not being merely mischievous; he is telling us something about how he thinks of music.

[65] Quoted in Bernard Aspell, "Glenn Gould," *Horizon* 4, no. 3 (January 1962), p. 92; and in Payzant, *Glenn Gould,* p. 105. By a curious inversion, his single recording on organ, of the first nine fugues from Bach's *The Art of the Fugue,* sound awfully piano-like.

[66] My transcription from the audio disc *Glenn Gould: Concert Dropout.*

[67] Heard, among other places, on *Glenn Gould: Concert Dropout.* Two other related anecdotes are labelled "The Last Resort" (Gould's own name for the expedient of turning on the vacuum or radio) and "The Half Hour" (Gould's claim that "everything there is to know about playing the piano can be taught in half an hour"; see Cott, *Conversations,* p. 31). This desert story also includes a backstage encounter with Kafka executor Max Brod and his female companion, who congratulate Gould on his recital of Beethoven's Second Concerto. The punchline, delivered in a heavy German accent, is that the woman calls it "unquestionably ze finest Mozart I haf ever heard!" (Cott, *Conversations,* p. 35).

[68] Payzant, *Glenn Gould,* p. 88. Payzant's larger discussion of musical idealism and the issues of tactility versus intellect in music is excellent; see chs. 5 and 6.

[69] Huizinga, *Homo Ludens,* p. 163.

[70] The best book I know on the play of taste and distinction in popular music is Carl Wilson's *Let's Talk About Love: A Journey to the End of Taste* (New York: Continuum, 2007), not least because of how Wilson, a music critic, manages to weave an analysis of Hume, Kant, Veblen, and Bourdieu through his personal engagement with the music of Céline Dion.

[71] It is not, perhaps, surprising that Bourdieu uses Clark as a handy example of "popular taste," distinct from both "middlebrow" (Gershwin's *Rhapsody in Blue*) and "legitimate" taste (Bach's *The Well-Tempered Clavier*). With Petula Clark, he says, we find "songs totally devoid of artistic ambition or pretension" (p. 16).

[72] *GGR,* p. 304.

[73] *GGR,* p. 323.

[74] Quoted in Bazzana, *Wondrous Strange,* p. 465; Friedrich, *Glenn Gould,* p. 225.

[75] *GGR,* p. 415.

[76] I thank Richler biographer Charles Foran for this quotation.

[77] In fact it is more complicated than that. Susan Sontag, in "Notes on Camp," *Partisan Review* (1964), suggests that camp is the refuge of the dandy in an age of mass culture, when traditional, hyper-refined aestheticism is no longer a viable option: "As the dandy is the nineteenth century's surrogate for the aristocrat in matters of culture, so Camp is the modern dandyism. Camp is the answer to the problem: how to be a dandy in the age of mass

culture" (note 45). Oscar Wilde is the key transitional figure between the high culture aesthete and the hi-lo reversals of the camp dandy. I would place Gould as the dark mirror-image of Wilde's brightness. He, too, marks the transition to mass culture and has the same preoccupations with aesthetics-as-ethics, though with an opposite valence. His avowed preferences for motels, diners, Detroit-built cars, and the music of Petula Clark may be read as his form of camp engagement with popular culture.

[78] *GGR*, p. 326.

[79] *GGR*, pp. 327–28.

[80] My transcription from the audio disc.

[81] My transcription from the audio disc.

[82] *GGR*, p. 390.

[83] For a sobering treatment of these issues, see Ken S. Coates et al., *Arctic Front: Defending Canada in the Far North* (Toronto: Thomas Allen, 2008). Coates and his colleagues argue for national policies that would integrate and support a distinctively Aboriginal north, best served by designation as a development-free zone, like the Antarctic.

[84] Anthony Storr, *The Dynamics of Creation* (1972; rev. ed. New York: Ballantine, 1993), p. 57; quoted and discussed in Payzant, *Glenn Gould,* p. 52 ff.

[85] *GGR*, pp. 445–46.

[86] *GGR*, p. 447.

[87] *GGR*, p. 448.

[88] See, for example, T.W. Adorno, *Philosophy of New Music* (1947; rev. ed. Minneapolis: University of Minnesota Press, 2007) and *Introduction to the Sociology of Music* (New York: Continuum, 1976); also Stanley Cavell, "Music Discomposed" and "A Matter of Meaning It," in his *Must We Mean What We Say?* (Cambridge: Cambridge University Press, 1969).

[89] See Payzant, *Glenn Gould,* ch. 8, for this illuminating discussion.

[90] I will not attempt to cite the vast philosophical literature on this topic, including psychoanalytic, critical theoretic, and existential works, but two books are worth singling out: Lionel Trilling, *Sincerity and Authenticity* (Cambridge, Mass.: Harvard University Press, 1972), which argues persuasively that we moderns are more concerned with authenticity (being true to oneself) than those in earlier eras, say, Shakespeare's Elizabethan time, when the central issue was sincerity in speech (being true to another); and Harry Frankfurt, *The Importance of What We Care About* (Cambridge: Cambridge University Press, 1988), which includes a crisp analytic treatment of the desire-ordering that goes into the human project of *wholeheartedness*. My thanks to Lauren Bialystok for discussion of these issues.

[91] *GGR,* p. 368.

[92] *GGR,* p. 354.

[93] *GGR,* p. 216.

[94] *GGR,* p. 219.

[95] Botstein, a violinist, essayist, and college administrator, articulates in a manner now almost unknown this strain of barbarians-at-the-

gates cultural critique; see his "Outside In: Music on Language," in Leonard Michaels and Christopher Ricks, eds., *The State of the Language* (Berkeley: University of California Press, 1980).

[96] This may be signalled by the sad fact that Stockhausen's clearest contemporary identity is that of the man who declared the 2001 attacks on New York's World Trade Center to be "the greatest work of art" imaginable. That he meant *art* in the sense of sublime Luciferian violence was naturally lost in the ensuing controversy.

[97] Jean-François Lyotard, *The Postmodern Condition: A Report on Knowledge* (1979; English trans. Geoff Bennington and Brian Massumi, Minneapolis: University of Minnesota Press, 1984). It is worth remembering that Lyotard's focus was neither technology nor art but knowledge. his argument is epistemological.

[98] See Arthur Danto, *Beyond the Brillo Box: The Visual Arts in Post-Historical Perspective* (Berkeley: University of California Press, 1998) and *After the End of Art: Contemporary Art and the Pale of History* (Princeton: Princeton University Press, 1998). Danto pegs the death of art to the year 1964 and the exhibition of work by Andy Warhol, that well-known Asperger sufferer, though one might think Duchamp's readymades had already hammered the spike in part way.

[99] *GGR,* p. 358.

[100] *GGR,* p. 355.

[101] *GGR,* p. 353.

[102] Notably that of Scarborough native Mike Myers: see *Shrek* and its sequels, the *Austin Powers* movies, *So I Married an Axe Murderer,*

and justly forgotten *Saturday Night Live* sketches about a store that sells only Scottish items, including the inherently hilarious foodstuff haggis.

[103] All quotations here are my transcriptions from the audio disc and liner notes.

[104] He is called Teddy Slotz in Jonathan Cott's 1974 conversation with Gould about the "doppelgänger syndrome" and tricksterism running through Gould's thought (first published in *Rolling Stone* magazine). Cott hazards that Slutz/Slotz is a takeoff of Lorin Hollander, the celebrated American pianist and conductor. Gould insists on his New York cabdriver provenance. To my ear, the closest cultural analogue is a somewhat obscure one: Slutz sounds like the drunken occult writer Sidney Redlitch, played by Ernie Kovacs in the 1958 witch-love comedy *Bell, Book, and Candle* (d. Richard Quine).

[105] Online amazon.com review.

[106] *GGR,* p. 399.

[107] Herbert Fingarette, "Insanity and Responsibility," *Inquiry* 15 (1972): 6–29.

[108] *GGR,* p. 309.

[109] The psychologist Jordan Peterson suggested this reading of Elvis Presley at a conference on new classical music (Royal Ontario Museum, 2005); the reading of Hughes as driven mad by post-modernity is nicely portrayed in Steven Carter's novel *I Was Howard Hughes* (New York: Bloomsbury, 2003).

[110] *GGR,* p. 47.

[111] The story is that Cage made his first version of the remark during a lecture about Erik Satie at Black Mountain College, North Carolina, in 1950. He then repeated it often, notably to the poet John Ashbery during a Manhattan cocktail party; Ashbery spread the tale further. In *The Rest Is Noise: Listening to the Twentieth Century* (New York: Farrar, Straus & Giroux, 2008), music critic Alex Ross's accessible account of music's later development, Cage's view is discussed as part of a general avant-gardiste turn in the United States during the 1950s; see ch. 14.

[112] My transcription of the liner notes; also *GGR,* p. 13.

[113] *GGR,* p. 447.

[114] *GGR,* p. 246, as part of the general argument of the 1962 essay "Let's Ban Applause," first published in the journal *Musical America;* also quoted in Payzant, *Glenn Gould,* p. 64.

[115] This promise may be disappointing as well as moving: see, for example, Alexander Nehemas, *Only a Promise of Happiness: The Place of Beauty in a World of Art* (Princeton: Princeton University Press, 2007) and, for an optimistic but finally unconvincing extension of the argument, Elaine Scarry, *On Beauty and Being Just* (Princeton: Princeton University Press, 1999).

ACKNOWLEDGMENTS

In writing about this remarkable artist I have tried to create a vision of his thought suitable to the contradictions and complicated pleasures of the post-historical world. Along the way I have been aided by many works: several useful biographies of the narrative kind, especially Kevin Bazzana, *Wondrous Strange: The Life and Art of Glenn Gould* (2004); Otto Friedrich, *Glenn Gould: A Life and Variations* (1989; 2002); and (advisedly) Peter Ostwald, *Glenn Gould: The Ecstasy and Tragedy of Genius* (1998); the indispensable *Glenn Gould Reader* (1984), edited by Tim Page; Jonathan Cott, *Conversations with Glenn Gould* (1984); and the illuminating early philosophical study by the late Geoffrey Payzant, *Glenn Gould, Music and Mind* (1978; 1984). I have not attempted to document, let alone assess, the vast volume of scholarly Gouldiana that grows by the year, but various books and articles of larger philosophical interest are cited in Sources.

My thanks to Diane Turbide at Penguin Canada and general editor John Ralston Saul for the opportunity to be part of the Extraordinary Canadians series. Esther Shubert provided extremely valuable aid with research, permissions, and proofing. The Glenn Gould Estate and Key Porter Books were generous with permission to quote directly from

Gould's published writings. Discussions with many friends have been useful, sometimes especially when not explicitly about music. A conversation and performance by Angela Hewitt in February 2009 clarified for me the ways in which interpreting J.S. Bach is so challenging and rewarding.

Small portions of this work appeared first in *The Globe and Mail* and in volume ten of *Alphabet City: Suspect* (Cambridge, Mass.: MIT Press, 2006). Audiences at the Royal Ontario Museum in Toronto (2005), Groningen University in the Netherlands (2008), Trinity College, University of Toronto (2008), and Cornell University (2009) listened patiently to early versions of some ideas and offered valuable feedback. Finally, my students in several recent seminars on philosophy of art have been important and I would like to think mostly willing participants in thinking about the mystery that is music. Thank you all.

All the words in this book were composed with Gould's music audible in the background. I do not count that as *listening*, except merely factually; but it may be understood as an optimistic osmotic gesture. Listening to Gould in a real sense—that is, playing every recorded piece of his at least three times and some, such as the 1981 *Goldberg Variations* and his single Byrd and Gibbons disc, too many times to count—has been the great gift of this project. In 2007

Columbia Records released a boxed compact disc set of every LP Gould recorded for them, reproduced with facsimile covers. This treasure is something no Gould fan can be without; in a perfect world a version of it would accompany each copy of this book.

1932   Glenn Herbert Gould is born on September 25
         to Russell Herbert Gould and Florence Emma
         Gould in their home at 32 Southwood Drive in
         the Beach, Toronto. He is their only child.

1938   At the age of five, Gould gives his first public
         performance for the thirtieth-anniversary
         celebration of the Business Men's Bible Class
         (of which Bert Gould was a member) in
         Uxbridge, Ontario, on June 5. He also accom-
         panied his parents' vocal duet.

1945   Gould makes his professional debut on organ
         at the Eaton Auditorium on December 12,
         playing Mendelssohn's Sonata no. 6, the
         Concerto Movement by Dupuis, and the
         Fugue in F Minor by J.S. Bach.

1946   After passing both his piano exams in June
         1945, with the highest marks of any candidate,
         and his written theory exams, Gould is
         awarded the Associate diploma at the Toronto
         Conservatory of Music (later the Royal
         Conservatory of Music) on October 28.

On May 8 Gould gives his first performance with an orchestra, playing the first movement of Beethoven's Concerto no. 4 at Massey Hall with the Conservatory Symphony Orchestra.

1947   Gould makes his professional debut on piano in the Secondary School Concerts series on January 14 and 15 with the Toronto Symphony Orchestra, playing all four movements of Beethoven's Concerto no. 4.

On October 20, Gould makes his official recital debut as a professional pianist at Eaton Auditorium as part of the International Artists series; the recital includes works by Scarlatti, Beethoven, Chopin, Liszt, and Mendelssohn.

1949   At age sixteen, Gould has his original work played in public for the first time, during a student performance of *Twelfth Night* by the Malvern Drama Club on February 18; he plays his own piano suite.

1950   On December 24 at 10:30 A.M. on the CBC, Gould gives his first professional radio broadcast, playing a Mozart sonata in B-flat Major [K 281] and a Hindemith Sonata in B-flat, op. 37. Gould recalled this event as the beginning of his "love affair with the microphone."

1952   The first public performance of the *Goldberg Variations* is broadcast on the CBC on June 21.

1953   Gould tapes his first commercial recording, of Berg's Sonata, at the Bloor Street United Church with Hallmark Records on November 3; this is also his first opportunity to publish writing, in the form of liner notes.

1955   Gould has his American debuts, in Washington, D.C. (January 2), and New York City (January 11), playing works by Gibbons, Sweenlinck, Webern, Beethoven, Berg, and J.S. Bach. The day after the New York performance, David Oppenheim, director of artists and repertoire for Columbia Records' Masterworks division, contacts Gould's manager to offer Gould an exclusive recording contract—the first time Columbia signs an artist based on one hearing.

Gould signs a three-year contract with Columbia on May 1, making him the first Canadian to sign with this label; he announces that he wants his first recording to be of the *Goldberg Variations*.

Gould records the *Goldberg Variations* in Columbia's 30th Street studios from June 10 to 15. Even before the album is released, word of Gould's talent and eccentricities spreads: the disc becomes the most anticipated recording debut in classical-music history.

1956   The *Goldberg Variations* is released in January— an instant popular and critical success.

On May 21, the world premiere of Gould's String Quartet in F Minor, op. 1, written between April 1953 and October 1955, is performed by the Montreal String Quartet on CBC's French radio network.

1957   During the summer, Gould embarks on his first overseas tour, beginning in the Soviet Union, the first Canadian musician and the first pianist from North America to appear in post-Stalinist Russia. His performances in Moscow and Leningrad are overwhelming successes. Among other stops Gould also performs in Berlin with the Berlin

Philharmonic, conducted by Herbert
von Karajan.

1958   After the first performance, in Salzburg, of
        Gould's second overseas tour in late summer
        through to winter, he complains of a cold
        due to the air conditioning. He feels well
        enough to perform in Brussels, Berlin, and
        Stockholm but cancels all performances for
        October, citing bronchitis. Later he describes
        his month-long stay in Hamburg as the best
        month of his life.

1959   During Gould's December 8 visit to Steinway
        in New York, chief technician William
        Hupfer playfully slaps Gould on the back.
        Soon after, Gould begins complaining of a
        major injury and begins daily orthopedic and
        chiropractic treatments. He also cancels three
        months of concerts, including a European
        tour scheduled for February 1960, and files
        suit against the company and Hupfer,
        demanding $300,000 in personal damages.

1960   Gould gives his first Canadian public
        performance of Schoenberg's Piano

Concerto with the Toronto Symphony
Orchestra in December.

1962   On August 8, Gould broadcasts his first
attempt at a radio documentary, *Arnold
Schoenberg: The Man Who Changed Music,*
on the CBC.

1964   Gould's last public performance is on April 10,
a recital in Los Angeles, where he plays four
fugues from Bach's The Art of the Fugue and
the Partita no. 4 in D Major, Beethoven's
Opus 109, and Hindemith's Third Sonata.

1965   In June, Gould takes CN Rail's Muskeg Express
to Churchill, Manitoba; while aboard he meets
and befriends Wally Maclean, a retired surveyor.
The trip becomes the inspiration for "The Idea
of North."

1967   "The Idea of North" is aired December 28
on the CBC Radio program *Ideas.* "The
Latecomers" (1969), about Newfoundland, and
"Quiet in the Land" (1977), about Mennonites,
complete the so-called *Solitude Trilogy.*

1974   Gould wins the only Grammy awarded in his
lifetime, for Best Album Notes—Classical

(*Hindemith: Sonatas for Piano,* performed by
Glenn Gould).

1975   On July 26 Gould's mother dies of a stroke at
eighty-three; unable to overcome anxiety about
hospital visits, Gould has final conversations
with her by telephone.

1979   Gould's film about Toronto, including
a scene of him singing Mahler to the
elephants at the Toronto Zoo, debuts on
September 29.

1979   Gould and French director Bruno Monsaingeon
begin filming a projected six-part work, *Glenn
Gould Plays Bach.*

The first Sony Walkman portable cassette
tape player is available for sale.

1980   *The Glenn Gould Silver Jubilee Album* is
released in August, celebrating his twenty-
fifth year as a Columbia recording artist; it
includes the bizarre piece "A Glenn Gould
Fantasy."

1981   Over six studio sessions from April through
May, Gould rerecords and films the *Goldberg
Variations* as the third instalment in *Glenn*

Gould Plays Bach; the film is shown in France on January 2, 1982.

1982   Gould completes his last recording sessions, of Wagner's *Siegfried Idyll,* at St. Lawrence Hall in Toronto from July 27 to 29.

Gould's second recording of the *Goldberg Variations* is released in September.

Gould suffers a severe headache and is admitted to the Toronto General Hospital at 8:44 P.M. on September 27; the preliminary diagnosis is a stroke with left-side paralysis caused by a blood clot.

On October 4, after Gould experiences further complications and evidence of brain damage is discovered, Gould's father decides to withdraw life support; Glenn Gould is pronounced dead at 11 A.M.

Compact discs become commercially available in October.

1983   Glenn Gould is inducted into the Canadian Music Hall of Fame. He wins a posthumous 1982 Grammy Award for Best Classical Album (*Bach: The Goldberg Variations*) and

Best Instrumental Soloist Performance (without orchestra) (*Bach: The Goldberg Variations*).

1984   Gould wins a third posthumous Grammy Award for Best Instrumental Soloist Performance (without orchestra) (*Beethoven: Piano Sonatas Nos. 12 and 13*).

1989   In April, the first patent is issued for MP3 format for compression of digital audio files.

1999   Starting in February, independent record company SubPop Records is the first to distribute music tracks in MP3 format.

Apple introduces the iPod portable MP3 player in November.

2007   On the seventy-fifth anniversary of Gould's birth and the twenty-fifth of his death, worldwide iPod sales top 100 million units.